Fire for Effect: *The Unproduced Screenplay*
© 2012 Ib Melchior. All Rights Reserved.

No part of this book may be reproduced in any form or by any means, electronic, mechanical, digital, photocopying or recording, except for the inclusion in a review, without permission in writing from the publisher.

Published in the USA by:
BearManor Media
PO Box 1129
Duncan, Oklahoma 73534-1129
www.bearmanormedia.com

ISBN 978-1-59393-726-3

Printed in the United States of America.
Book design by Brian Pearce | Red Jacket Press.

INTRODUCTION

Fire For Effect is a WWII story, but not of the ordinary kind. It involves a vitally important, but little known, branch of Military Intelligence — the IPWs — the Interrogators of Prisoners of War. It is the story of a battle of wits between two officers, good men both, with strong convictions, integrity and a firm sense of duty — but on opposite sides, and it concerns a potentially catastrophic event about to happen. It is solved without either of the two men compromising his integrity. It is based on a true incident, the location is factual and the character of the IPW is based on the officer who lived the story and was decorated for his achievement, Leo Handel.

I met Leo when we both attended Military Intelligence School back in 1942. When I saw him I thought he looked like the most stuck-up, fatuous guy I'd ever seen. Later I found out that that was exactly what he had thought of me — naturally we had to become fast friends — a friendship that lasted until Leo passed away at 90. I think of him as the best friend I ever had. After graduation from Military Intelligence School we went our separate ways in the army. I was sent to Germany and worked as an agent with the CIC — Counter Intelligence Corps, and Leo went to Italy as an IPW. But we kept in touch, even managed to keep each other informed of where we were and what we were doing, although it was strictly forbidden to write about such potentially damaging information should the correspondence fall into enemy hands. We did it by devising a simple but unsolvable code, which only the two of us knew. It was based on the beginning and end of the letter, how we greeted each other and how we signed off. For example, "Dear Leo" meant — *I am in Germany;* "Hi Leo" meant — *I am in Italy;* "Hi Buddy" meant — *I am in Africa;* and "Hi Good Buddy" meant — *I am stuck in England.* And in signing off, "Your Buddy" meant — *I am in CIC, working in a rear echelon HQ,* while "Your Good Buddy" meant — *I work as a CIC agent with the front line troops;* "Best regards" meant — *I am an IPW with the front line troops.* "So Long" meant — *I am working in the war room,* and if there were a PS of any kind, it meant — *I was wounded but am OK.* That way, we had a good idea of what we were doing — but nobody else did! Friend or foe…

Both Leo and I wanted to make motion pictures in Hollywood — and after the war, we both did. *Fire For Effect* would have been a film we would have made together. We never got around to getting our teeth into it and finding a studio willing to take it on. When Leo died — much too soon — I did not want to try to make the film without him, it somehow felt "incomplete." Consequently it was not "shown around," but I now realize that the film is a tribute to Leo's achievement, which should be told.

Ib Melchior

FIRE FOR EFFECT

OGIGINAL SCREENPLAY
BY

IB MELCHIOR

Reg WGAW

The Coppage Company
3369 Canton Lane
Studio City, CA 91604
(818) 980-8806

FIRE FOR EFFECT...

...IS THE ACTION-PACKED STORY OF A VITALLY IMPORTANT WAR-TIME ARTILLERY DUEL. BUT EVEN MORE SIGNIFICANTLY IT IS THE STORY OF AN EXCITING DUEL BETWEEN TWO OFFICERS; GOOD MEN BOTH, WITH STRONG CONVICTIONS, INTEGRITY AND SENSE OF DUTY - BUT ON OPPOSITE SIDES... A DUEL OF WITS, PERSONAL COURAGE AND DEEP IDEOLOGIES...

FIRE FOR EFFECT

CAST LIST

UNITED STATES ARMY

    Capt. Dirk Parker, IPW
    Maj. Paul Armstrong, Regimental S-2
    Col. Henry Bradford, Regimental C.O.
    Sgt. Jim Hicks, IPW
    Sgt. Davis
    Pfc. Alvin Coffman
    Capt. Stern, U.S.A. Medical Corps
    Sgt. Mike Ryan
    Pfc. Johnny Bell

    Officers, Non-Coms and G.I.'s (Romeo, Sam, Pinto)
    Red Cross Girls (Susie, Joanie)

GERMAN WEHRMACHT

    Lt. Otto Heinrich, Air Corps Artillery Observer
    Maj. Rudolf Schiller
    Obergef. Hans Richter
    Gef. Johann Kovacheck, PW

    Officers, Non-Coms and Soldiers (Cpl. Krim)

ITALIAN PARTISANS

    Rina
    "Volpe," Partisan Leader
    Tony
    Partisans: Civilians for general atmosphere
    Luigi

"FIRE FOR EFFECT"

         FADE IN:

EXT. RUINS OF SANTA ANGELO VILLAGE   NIGHT

1   SHOT

     It is the rubble-strewn outskirts of the little village.
     Shelled, bombed, evacuated Santa Angelo - hardly bigger
     than a good-sized farm - is located high on the SW slope
     of Monte Adone in Italy.

2   CLOSE SHOT   PAN

     We see a small, wooden roadside shrine so common in many
     European countries. Under the V-shaped roof stands a
     carved figure of the Madonna. Her arms are gently, lovingly
     cradled in front of her, and she is serenely gazing down
     at the child resting there.

     CAMERA SLOWLY PANS OFF the shrine, across the ruins of a
     stone shack to a pile of rubble and debris. In a CLOSE
     SHOT in f.g. lies a big piece of broken masonry. Slowly a
     dirty hand snakes over the brick, and the roundness of a
     U.S. Army steel helmet is cautiously raised over the rim.
     A pair of alert, watchful eyes, set in a grimy face, peers
     over the rubble.

3   ANOTHER WIDER ANGLE

     Lying prone behind the masonry - rifle cradled in his arms
     - SERGEANT MIKE RYAN is cautiously surveying the dark, dead,
     deserted ruins of the little village.

4   LONG SHOT   SANTA ANGELO VILLAGE

     It is dark and deserted.

5   MED. SHOT   FEATURING SGT. RYAN

     Having satisfied himself he makes a "forward" motion with
     his arm, and silently he bellies around the rubble to
     another place of cover. Several other silent, shadowy
     figures can be seen, strung out behind him, noiselessly
     crawling on, following Ryan.

6   ANOTHER ANGLE

Ryan stops behind a piece of toppled stone wall. He motions to a G.I. near him. Quickly, noiselessly, the man, PFC JOHNNY BELL, crawls over to join the Sergeant. With a whisper Ryan turns to him:

>   RYAN
>   (in a whisper)
>   Pass it on. Watch out for booby
>   traps. The place must be lousy
>   with the damned things.
>
>   JOHNNY
>   Okay.

He starts away. Ryan creeps on.

7   CLOSER ANGLE   RYAN

He is snaking across the rubble.

8   ANOTHER ANGLE   WIDER SHOT   TWO G.I.s

They are carefully, silently infiltrating from cover to cover. Johnny comes crawling up to one of them. He whispers to him. The man nods and starts towards the other G.I.

9   WIDE SHOT

The patrol is silently advancing; the men are cautiously picking their way, taking expert advantage of every bit of cover.

10   MED. CLOSE SHOT   YOUNG G.I.

He is bellying across the broken masonry and other debris towards CAMERA - and towards the corner of a bombed-out building. Down the cracked wall in f.g. runs an old rusty drain pipe; on the ground lies a half-broken flagstone. Silently the G.I. is crawling towards it - and CAMERA.

The moon briefly stabs its pale rays through a rift in the cloud cover - and the sudden, quick glint of metal flashes from a thin wire running from the broken flagstone to the drain pipe...and the shadows close in again.

Slowly the soldier nears the stone; carefully he places one hand on the edge of it, and pushing forward he puts his weight on it....

(CONTINUED)

10   CONTINUED:

Instantly there is a blinding flash and the shock of an explosion. The drain pipe blows asunder, showering the soldier and the ground around him with flaming gasoline!

With a hideous SCREAM the man rolls on the burning ground, his hands covering his face, his clothes ablaze...

11   WIDE SHOT

At once Sergeant Ryan and Johnny - forgetting their own danger - leap to their feet and sprint for their comrade. Ryan barks out a command to the others of the patrol even as he runs to the aid of the writhing G.I.

     RYAN
  Stay put! Don't move!

12   CLOSER ANGLE

Ryan and Johnny get to the trapped G.I.; they drag him away from the blazing gasoline on the ground and frantically beat at his flaming clothes, while the other patrol members look on aghast...

     RYAN
    (to Johnny)
  Smother it!

The two men begin to heap dirt over the flames with their bare hands.

13   CLOSE SHOT   RYAN

He is shovelling dirt; the flames from the burning soldier are mirrored on his horrified face...

14   CLOSEUP   PATROL MEMBER

Lying in cover he is watching the terrible scene; he turns his face away.

15   THREE SHOT   RYAN, JOHNNY, G.I.

Ryan and Johnny are working desperately to put out the flames still leaping from the tortured man; in the b.g. the ground is ablaze with burning gasoline.

16 CLOSEUP SOLDIER

The tortured boy's face is distorted with fear and agony; quickly CAMERA ZOOMS IN to an EXTREME CLOSEUP of the soldier's eyes, forced wide open, straining in anguish as if to leave their very sockets...

                                        MATCH CUT TO:

EXT. GERMAN OBSERVATION POST ON THE SLOPE OF MONTE ADONE   NIGHT

17 EXTREME CLOSEUP   GERMAN FIELD GLASSES

Dancing in the two lenses are the tiniest specks of flame. CAMERA QUICKLY ZOOMS OUT to a MED. SHOT of a German Air Corps Artillery Observer, LT. OTTO HEINRICH. Hidden in the O.P. he is intently looking through the field glasses. Quickly he lowers them and at once rings a field telephone. Almost immediately he snaps into it:

                HEINRICH
              (on phone)
        Enemy patrol in Santa Angelo! Fire
        one round!

Again he looks through the field glasses; within seconds the ominous whine of an artillery shell passing overhead is HEARD - and then the distant impact EXPLOSION. Heinrich barks on the phone:

                HEINRICH
              (on phone)
        Up 200. Fire for effect!

EXT. GERMAN ARTILLERY POSITION   NIGHT

18 WIDE SHOT (STOCK)

It is a battery of 88's. The position is located in a mountainous area. The guns are firing an ear-splitting salvo.

From the flame and smoke spewing gun muzzles explodes the MAIN TITLE:

        F I R E   F O R   E F F E C T

19 ANOTHER ANGLE (STOCK)

The battery fires again; the roar of sound is marrow-freezing.

EXT. RUINS OF SANTA ANGELO VILLAGE   NIGHT

20   MED. WIDE SHOT

A shell lands near Ryan and Johnny, still tending the wounded G.I.; they hit the ground instantaneously. Another shell lands, showering them with dirt and debirs.

21   VARIOUS SHOTS OF A SMALL ITALIAN VILLAGE BEING SHELLED (STOCK)

The patrol is caught in the village. The shells drop with marrow-freezing explosions and geysers of death-dealing flame, steel fragments and dirt all around them...and each new explosion brings with it a CREDIT, as the deadly barrage falls on the little village...

As the last CREDIT FADES OUT, the terrifying barrage dies down. The battered, tortured battlefield lies still and silent; wispy smoke spirals rise lazily from the rubble - the only movement to be seen...

                                    SLOW DISSOLVE:

INT. IPW ROOM OF SANTA MARIA SCHOOL HOUSE   NIGHT

22   CLOSE SHOT   MAP OF ITALY

The map shows the German and Allied frontline positions, as they were at the end of March, 1945.

> NARRATOR
> Italy, March, 1945. The Allied Forces were bracing themselves for the Big Push. Objective: The Po Valley, food basket of Italy; now supply bin for the German Wehrmacht.

23   MONTAGE SUPERIMPOSED OVER MAP   VARIOUS STOCK SHOTS (U.S. ARMY)

The shots will be synchronized with the narration below:

a) Frontline positions
b) Guns - not firing
c) Army trucks moving up
d) Troops moving up
e) Ammunition dump
f) Tanks on tank transport trailers moving up
g) General activity

During the narration CAMERA SLOWLY DOLLIES IN to a CLOSER SHOT of a section of the front held by the American Fifth Army.

                                      (CONTINUED)

23 CONTINUED:

Clearly we see a small village called SANTA MARIA in the center of the area; a mountain named MONTE ADONE with a tiny village, SANTA ANGELO, marked on its SW slope. On the German side of the lines a few more villages can be seen.

      NARRATOR
  The frontlines lay sprawled like
  a restless giant across the Peninsula.
  The enemy held commanding peaks from
  the Ligurian Coast to the East, where
  the American Fifth Army rubbed
  shoulders with the British Eighth...
  Energy was stored up for the knockout
  punch. Reinforcements flowed in.
  Ammunition was stockpiled; supplies
  built up; new weapons added - prior
  to a decisive, full scale offensive...

The narration and montage finished, CAMERA HOLDS on the map. O.s. a sharp VOICE barks a command:

      VOICE (o.s.)
  Get your hands up. Get 'em up!

- and across the map falls the shadow of a pair of hands shooting into the air and held high.

24 WIDE SHOT

The room used by the Interrogation of Prisoners of War Team - IPW Team - is obviously located in the school of the small Italian village. There is a table and a blackboard, to which the large map is pinned, at one end of the room. The little desks for the now-absent pupils are telescoped hurriedly at the opposite end. Superimposed on the simple schoolroom furniture are all kinds of U.S. Army equipment including: A small filing cabinet, a field telephone in a leather case with a wire leading out the window. A pot bellied stove provides heat. Somewhere in the room we see a field cot with a bedroll spread over it. From a hook on the wall hangs an open Valpack. The same hook also suspends an open messkit complete with spoon, knife and fork. The windows have blackout curtains pulled across them to keep the light from the bright lamp from spilling out into the dark night. In a corner, incongruous to its environment, stands a huge, ornately carved grandfather clock. It has a distinctive dial, two weights and a pendulum swinging back and forth; CHIMES indicate the time every fifteen minutes. It is now a few minutes before ten o'clock...

          (CONTINUED)

24   CONTINUED:

It is a tense scene. CAPTAIN DIRK PARKER, C.O. of the IPW Team, is standing before a frightened looking man, a PW, JOHANN KOVACHECK. At the closed door stands SERGEANT JIM HICKS - alert and watchful. Kovacheck's uniform jacket and shirt lie over the back of a chair; he wears a dirty, torn undershirt, and his bare arms are held over his head...

Slowly, ominously Parker advances upon the trembling PW.

25   TWO SHOT   KOVACHECK, PARKER

> PARKER
> What's your blood type, soldier?
>
> KOVACHECK
> I - I don't know...

Suddenly Parker grabs the man's left arm and glances at the inside of it.

> KOVACHECK
> I am not SS, Captain. I have no tattoo!
>
> PARKER
> (drily)
> You're lucky! Take your arms down.

Kovacheck obeys - relieved. Parker returns to his table.

> PARKER
> Put your clothes on.

Kovacheck snaps to.

> KOVACHECK
> Yes, sir!

He hurries to obey. Parker picks up a few personal items from his table, belonging to Kovacheck. He looks them over: A few currency bills; some coins; a small photograph of a smiling girl with an inscription on it; a small screw-type can opener; a stubby pencil.

> PARKER
> Alright, Kovacheck. Once again. What is your unit?
>
> KOVACHECK
> (snapping to; reciting for the umpteenth time)
> Johann Kovacheck, Gefreiter, 205-044-262.

(CONTINUED)

25   CONTINUED:

> PARKER
> (bored)
> Name, rank and serial number. That's all you have to say?

> KOVACHECK
> Jawohl, Herr Captain.

> PARKER
> I see.
> (he looks speculatively at the PW)
> Well - it's your decision.

Parker hands Kovacheck his things - keeping the photo.

> PARKER
> Here are your things.

He looks at the photo and reads the inscription.

> PARKER
> (continues)
> "To my Johann. My heart goes with you. Lotte." - Lovely girl. Your wife?

Kovacheck starts to answer - but checks himself. He remains silent.

> PARKER
> Girl friend, then?

Kovacheck does not answer. Parker turns the photo over. There is a little stamp on the back of it. Parker reads it.

> PARKER
> "Foto Kleinert. Teplitz-Schönau"... Teplitz. That's in Czechoslovakia -- right?

He looks at Kovacheck; Kovacheck clamps his teeth together.

> PARKER
> (confidentially)
> You know, Kovacheck, I can't understand your attitude. You're not even a German.

> KOVACHECK
> (heatedly)
> I am, sir. A Sudeten German!

> PARKER
> Oh? Then Teplitz _is_ your home town.

(CONTINUED)

25 CONTINUED: - 2

   Kovacheck looks mortified; he hadn't meant to give any information. Parker glances at Hicks.

26 CLOSEUP   HICKS

   He nods imperceptibly.

27 TWO SHOT   PARKER, KOVACHECK

   Parker seems to lose interest in Kovacheck; he apparently is resigned to not getting any military information out of him.

                    PARKER
           Well, Kovacheck, are you going to
           tell me about your unit?

                    KOVACHECK
           No, sir.

                    PARKER
           Alright. If you insist on being
           uncooperative, there's nothing I
           can do. I'm sorry for you.

   Kovacheck looks puzzled at this cryptic remark. Parker turns to Hicks. CAMERA WIDENS TO INCLUDE HIM.

                    PARKER
           Sergeant. Let me have his Prisoner
           of War tag.

                    HICKS
           Yes, sir.

   Hicks goes up to Kovacheck and removes a large tag hanging from a button on his uniform coat. He gives it to Parker, who has taken a big grease pencil from the table drawer. With elaborate care he prints a huge "R" across the face of the tag. Kovacheck looks on apprehensively. Parker hands the tag to Hicks.

                    PARKER
           Here's another one for you, Sergeant.
           Take him away.

   Hicks takes the tag.

                    HICKS
           They'll be happy, sir. Him being
           born a Czech and all!

   He hangs the marked tag on Kovacheck.

                              (CONTINUED)

27 CONTINUED:

                    HICKS
    Come on!
           (under his breath)
    You poor slob...

He starts to herd Kovacheck towards the door. Kovacheck looks at the marked tag with a worried frown. At the door he stops - and turns to Parker, who has busied himself at the table.

                    KOVACHECK
    Pardon me, Herr Officer!

                    PARKER
           (after a pause;
            without looking up)
    What is it?

                    KOVACHECK
           (worriedly)
    Pardon me, what means this "R?"

                    PARKER
           (crisply)
    Russia!

28 CLOSEUP   KOVACHECK

He looks stunned; he wets his lips.

                    KOVACHECK
    Russia!

29 MED. THREE SHOT

                    KOVACHECK
    Please, Captain -- Why - Russia?

Parker looks up casually.

                    PARKER
    It's quite simple. It means you'll
    be turned over to the Russians for -
    eh - internment. I think their camps
    are somewhere in Siberia...

                    KOVACHECK
           (white-faced)
    But...why?

                    PARKER
    We have to send them a certain quota
    of our PW's -
            (MORE)

                                      (CONTINUED)

29   CONTINUED:

                    PARKER (CONT'D)
            Naturally we sent them the....
            uncooperative ones.
                    (he looks speculatively
                     at the man; with pity)
            Of course, Kovacheck, you being a
            Czech - a fellow Slav, so to speak -
            won't help you much with the Russians.

    Unconcernedly, he returns to his papers.

30   CLOSE SHOT   KOVACHECK

    He looks pale and frightened; again he runs his tongue
    over dry lips. Finally...

                    KOVACHECK
                        (beaten)
            What will the Herr Officer want to
            know?

    At once Parker's casual attitude changes; he becomes
    brusque, sharp and authoritative; his questions are fired
    like bullets.

                    PARKER
            Your unit?

    There is only a slight hesitation...

                    KOVACHECK
            173rd Engineer Battalion.

                    PARKER
            Company?

                    KOVACHECK
            2nd Company, 3rd Platoon.

                    PARKER
            What was your mission, when you
            were captured?

    Kovacheck hesitates. Parker at once turns to Hicks.

                    PARKER
                        (sharply)
            Sergeant!

                    KOVACHECK
                        (quickly)
            A mine field, Captain. We were
            laying a mine field.

                                            (CONTINUED)

30   CONTINUED:

Parker swings the map on his table around to face the prisoner.

                  PARKER
     Come here.

Kovacheck walks to the table.

                  PARKER
     Show me where.

Kovacheck studies the map; he points.

                  KOVACHECK
     This area. There.

                  PARKER
     On the SE slope of Monte Adone?

                  KOVACHECK
     Yes, sir.

                  PARKER
     Pattern?

                  KOVACHECK
     Regulation, sir.

                  PARKER
          (matter-of-factly)
     Your company has nine light machine
     guns and one 20 mm anti-tank gun at
     normal strength. What have you got now?

Kovacheck looks at Parker, astonished at his knowledge.

                  KOVACHECK
     Five machine guns.

                  PARKER
     That's all?

                  KOVACHECK
     Yes.

                  PARKER
     Where are they placed to cover the
     field?

Kovacheck bends over the map; he begins to point out the five positions. Parker hardly looks; he glances at Hicks; the two men seem to tense a little; we get the feeling that a vital, all-important question is about to be asked.

31 CLOSE SHOT   HICKS

He moves a little closer.

32 THREE SHOT

Kovacheck has pointed out the positions; he straightens up.

>   PARKER
>   (perhaps a shade
>   too casually)
>   Where is the artillery battery
>   located?

Kovacheck looks up in surprise.

>   KOVACHECK
>   Pardon, Captain?

>   PARKER
>   (sharply)
>   The artillery battery. The 88's.
>   Where is it located?

>   KOVACHECK
>   (nervously)
>   88's? I - I don't know, Herr
>   Captain.

>   PARKER
>   Don't start to play games now,
>   Kovacheck!

>   KOVACHECK
>   (getting increasingly
>   worried)
>   But please, Sir, I don't know. I
>   tell you anything - but I don't know...

>   PARKER
>   (sarcastically)
>   Are you trying to make me believe you
>   don't <u>know</u> about the 88's?

>   KOVACHECK
>   (confused)
>   Yes - I mean - NO, Captain, I do -
>   I mean, I have heard them firing -
>   I don't know where they are!

>   PARKER
>   (to Hicks)
>   Sergeant. Take him away. He seems
>   to have lost his memory all of a
>   sudden.

(CONTINUED)

32   CONTINUED:

Hicks takes hold of Kovacheck roughly.

> HICKS
> (firmly)
> Come on. Let's go!

> KOVACHECK
> (imploring)
> Please, Herr Captain, I don't know.
> I tell you. Believe me, I don't
> know.

> PARKER
> (coldly)
> We'll give you a little time to
> remember, Kovacheck. If I were you,
> I'd try. Hard!

He gives a nod of dismissal; Hicks pushes Kovacheck towards the door; the PW looks frightened as he leaves with the Sergeant.

33   CLOSE SHOT   PARKER

Unconsciously he sighs deeply. Then he pulls out an overlay and places it over the map. On it all the positions pointed out by Kovacheck are already marked. Parker lights a cigarette, as Hicks returns. With a grin the Sergeant goes over to the big grandfather clock; during the following he checks it against his watch and sets it two minutes ahead.

> HICKS
> Well - it worked again. You got
> him to talk.

> PARKER
> But not about the right things.

> HICKS
> Seems they all prefer us "decadent
> democrats" to the "savage Slavs!"

> PARKER
> (drily)
> Wouldn't you?

> HICKS
> I wonder how he'll feel, when he
> finds out that "Russian quota" story
> of yours is just a lot of baloney?

Parker grins; he begins to write out his report.

34   CLOSE SHOT   HICKS

He's putting on a little "show."

                    HICKS
          Ah - for the life of the IPW..."And
          what did you do in the big war, daddy?"
          "I was an IPW, son." "An I.P. - what?"
          "An Interrogator of Prisoners of War,
          sonny." "Yeah - but what did you do?"
          "Why - I made up stories and asked
          questions!" "Oh. Like our kindergarten
          teacher!"

He walks over to the table. CAMERA CARRIES him to a TWO SHOT.

                    HICKS
          Did he come up with anything new?

                    PARKER
          Not a thing. Just confirmed what
          we already know.
                    (tensely)
          Hicks. We've got to find those 88's.
          Where the hell are they?!

                    HICKS
          Yeah. Bradford's looking to bust a
          gut.

                    PARKER
          Damned thing is, he didn't know.
          He was telling the truth all the
          way down the line. I got him to
          talk just to set him up for the
          jackpot question.

                    HICKS
          And came up with three lemons!

He looks at the big clock.

                    HICKS
          Jim Ryan's patrol is about due back.
          Maybe they'll bring some fresh meat...

Suddenly - from outside the building - there is the distant cry of "Medic!" "Medic!"

Parker and Hicks look at one another - then they hurry from the room...

EXT. SANTA MARIA VILLAGE SQUARE   NIGHT

35   LONG SHOT

It is a typical Italian village square. In the center is a small stone fountain; several of the houses show the cruel damage of war; a few U.S. Army vehicles are parked around the streets; several signs point the way to the various organic units of the 89th Mountain Infantry Regiment, the C.P. of which is located in the school house, the most substantial building left undamaged in Santa Maria.

Parker and Hicks come hurrying from the school house; they stop and look around...

36   TWO SHOT   PARKER AND HICKS

They are looking off...

37   LONG SHOT   POV   PARKER AND HICKS

Down one of the streets leading from the square. A sign over a building indicates the Regimental Aid Station. A few G.I.'s can be seen approaching the building; two of them carry a stretcher made of two M-1 rifles and two coats; on it lies a still figure.

38   SHOT ACROSS PARKER AND HICKS TO AID STATION IN B.G.

Parker and Hicks take off for the Aid Station, as the soldiers enter the building with the stretcher...Parker and Hicks get to the house and hurry in...

INT. REGIMENTAL AID STATION   NIGHT

39   MED. WIDE SHOT

It is the receiving room of the Aid Station; it is nearly bare of furniture and brightly lit. The man on the makeshift litter has been placed on a cot; a medical officer, CAPTAIN STERN, is examining him aided by a medical orderly; during the following Stern and his aides work over the wounded man; the G.I.'s stand around - silently and soberly.

Parker and Hicks come in.

                    STERN
                (to orderly)
    Plasma!

Without a word the orderly efficiently moves to set up the plasma stand; Stern is giving the as yet unseen soldier on the cot a morphine shot.

40 CLOSER ANGLE

Parker walks up to Stern. Hicks goes to talk quietly with the G.I.'s.

                    PARKER
              How is he?

Stern slowly shakes his head; then he moves - and we see the man on the stretcher. It is Sergeant Ryan. He is obviously badly wounded; a blood-soaked bandage is tied around his throat; his eyes are closed in his cut and bruised face - and he is breathing heavily.

                    STERN
                 (to other orderly)
              Get surgery ready!

Hicks joins Parker; he looks shaken. Parker glances at him - then, as he sees his expression, he turns to him.

                    PARKER
                 (to Hicks)
              The others?

Slowly, unbelievingly, Hicks shakes his head.

                    HICKS
                 (in a low voice)
              The whole patrol...The whole damned
              patrol..!

There is a sudden low moan from Ryan; the men turn to him. Ryan's eyes are open - he is obviously trying to say something, but the wound in his throat muffles it. Gravely Parker bends over the injured man. He speaks gently:

                    PARKER
              Take it easy, Ryan. You'll be okay.
              Looks like you got yourself a
              stateside ticket!

Ryan looks up at him almost pleadingly; he is trying to tell him something - but does not succeed.

                    PARKER
                 (realizing what Ryan
                  is trying to do)
              What happened? Where? Where did
              it happen?

With a great effort Ryan manages a barely audible whisper.

                    RYAN
              Trap...trapped...

                                            (CONTINUED)

40 CONTINUED:

The deep gash in his throat makes it impossible for him to go on; the morphine is taking effect - he closes his eyes.. Stern puts his hand on Parker's shoulder.

> STERN
> Sorry, Parker!...

Parker stands up; Stern motions to his two medical orderlies.

> STERN
> Take him in.

The men lift the stretcher up and go with it through the door to the next room. On the door hangs a sign with a Red Cross and the words: AID STATION.

> PARKER
> (to Stern)
> What're his chances?

> STERN
> (his manner is almost
> angry - not at any
> one, but at the whole
> damned mess)
> I don't know how in hell he made it back to the lines. He needs major surgery. He'll have to be evacuated at once - if he is to live. All I can do here is clean him up a bit.

And as Parker and Hicks look after him, he strides to the Aid Station room.

41 CLOSER ANGLE

Stern opens the door marked with the Aid Station; he goes in - and closes the door...

MATCH CUT TO:

EXT. STREET OUTSIDE AID STATION   NIGHT

42 MED. SHOT   REAR OF U.S. ARMY AMBULANCE

The doors - marked with big Red Crosses - are being opened. CAMERA PULLS BACK. A stretcher with Sergeant Ryan is being placed in the ambulance - and the doors are closed again.

As Parker and Hicks watch, the ambulance speeds off down the narrow street of Santa Maria.

43   CLOSEUP PARKER

He is looking after the ambulance with a worried frown.

44   MED. WIDE SHOT   PAN SHOT

Parker and Hicks start away, walking towards the school house; CAMERA PANS THEM to a LONG SHOT, as they walk off... They pass a jeep parked in the square, out of the way - and CAMERA HOLDS on the jeep.

45   CLOSER ANGLE   JEEP

The motor is running, although the jeep is standing still; behind the wheel sits a G.I. - PFC ALVIN COFFMAN; he is looking at the dashboard gauges intently; on the ground, watching him with fascination, sit a dog and a BOY; the boy wears a U.S. Army steel helmet without the liner; it sinks well down over his head. Alvin bangs with his fist on the dashboard.

                    BOY
                (hopefully)
        Now okay?

                    ALVIN
        Okay, Loo-wee-gee. Right on the button!

Alvin kills the motor, and the boy, LUIGI, scrambles to his feet; he pulls the helmet from his head - and CAMERA CARRIES HIM, as he eagerly scoots to the front of the jeep. Here he places the helmet, bowl-like, under the jeep radiator, picks up a wrench and - crouching down - reaches under the jeep...

46   CLOSEUP   DOG

He is watching curiously; he cocks his head.

47   CLOSE SHOT   LUIGI

With the wrench he gives the radiator drain cock a turn - and at once nice, hot, steaming water pours out to fill the helmet. Quickly Luigi closes the cock, and cradling the helmet carefully in both hands he carries it to Alvin and puts it on the ground next to the jeep.

                    ALVIN
        Good boy!

Alvin swings his legs out of the jeep, and we see he has removed his shoes and socks and rolled up his pants.

(CONTINUED)

47   CONTINUED:

He sits himself down on the side of the jeep floor and with a big sigh of utter contentment he places both his large feet in the steaming, hot water in the helmet!

                    ALVIN
          Ahhhhh!...

48   CLOSEUP   LUIGI

He grins a huge grin.

49   MED. SHOT

Alvin takes a cake of soap from his jacket pocket and vigorously begins to scrub his feet...

50   CLOSEUP   DOG

Again he cocks his head, as he watches Alvin; then he - "laughs!"

51   CLOSE SHOT   ALVIN'S FEET IN HELMET

Luxuriously Alvin is wriggling his toes in the steaming, hot soapy water...

                                        MATCH CUT TO:

INT. IPW ROOM OF SANTA MARIA SCHOOL HOUSE   NIGHT

52   CLOSE SHOT   CANTEEN CUP

Standing on top of the pot bellied stove it is full of steaming, hot coffee - being stirred by a messkit fork. CAMERA PULLS OUT to a MED. SHOT, revealing Parker, COL. HENRY BRADFORD, Regimental C.O. and MAJOR PAUL ARMSTRONG, Regimental S-2.

Bradford picks up the cup; he takes a sip; it is scalding hot; he joins the other two men at the blackboard, where they are looking at the area map, tacked up next to the map of Italy.

                    BRADFORD
          Dirk - I'll give it to you straight.
          Army's getting into the act. They
          want those confounded guns out of the
          way! Now - where is that battery?

                                        (CONTINUED)

52 CONTINUED:

> PARKER
> What's "air" doing about it, sir?

> ARMSTRONG
> Some recon planes yesterday. All negative.

> BRADFORD
> Our own artillery cubs have scouted the entire area. The boys took all kinds of chances. No 88's.
> (disgusted)
> You can't tell a tiger tank from a mule's rump in that rugged mess!

Bradford drinks his coffee, during:

> ARMSTRONG
> (importantly)
> They're masters at camouflage. You've got to give them credit for that.

> PARKER
> A talent born of necessity, I'd say...

> BRADFORD
> Army is putting pressure on Corps. Corps is putting pressure on Division. Division is putting pressure on me...
> (he looks straight at Parker)
> ..and I...

> PARKER
> (with a mirthless grin)
> Yes, sir! I know.

> BRADFORD
> (seriously)
> But here's something you don't know. Those 88's must be located - and destroyed. It's not because of those few rounds they lop over every night. It's a damned sight more important than that!

He turns to the map and indicates the areas, as he talks. Parker and Armstrong watch.

> BRADFORD
> We're getting set for the Big Push!

(CONTINUED)

52   CONTINUED: - 2

                PARKER
When, sir?

              BRADFORD
Word just got down from Division. D-Day in four days...Now - we'll have to mount our effort right through here - right through Santa Maria. The only possible approach.
      (he turns to Parker)
Corps Forward is moving into the village in two days. Their Command Post'll be set up here in the school house. Two days, Dirk! Those 88's'll <u>have</u> to be knocked out before then!

              PARKER
I have no leads at all, sir. I've had only one PW in the last couple of weeks.

              BRADFORD
And he knew nothing...

              PARKER
Nothing.

              ARMSTRONG
What about the paysans? There always seem to be some of them crossing the lines.
      (insinuatingly; to Parker)
Have you thought of trying them?

              PARKER
It's pretty well bottled up, Major. There've been no civilians crossing for over three weeks...I thought you knew..!

Armstrong clamps his teeth in mortification.

              BRADFORD
Well, we've <u>got</u> to find that battery. Those 88's can dump a full scale barrage right in our lap anytime they want to - break up the whole confounded offensive!

              PARKER
If I could get a couple of fresh PW's, sir...

                              (CONTINUED)

52   CONTINUED: - 3

Bradford turns to Armstrong.

>   BRADFORD
>   Armstrong - make sure another recon
>   patrol goes out tomorrow night.
>
>   ARMSTRONG
>   Yes, sir. But you know what happens.
>   Either they come back without
>   prisoners - or they don't come back
>   at all.
>
>   BRADFORD
>   Then this time - make it a combat
>   patrol...in force!
>
>   PARKER
>   Just get me a prisoner or two...

Bradford goes to the stove; he opens a C-ration can and makes himself another cup of coffee, during the following scene.

>   ARMSTRONG
>   (goading)
>   And are you sure you'd know what
>   to do, if we got you a prisoner?
>
>   PARKER
>   (keeping his temper
>   only with an effort)
>   I think so, sir.

Armstrong raises a disdainful eyebrow. We feel the antagonism between the two men as an almost tangible thing.

>   ARMSTRONG
>   You didn't get anything out of the
>   last one..
>
>   PARKER
>   For a very good reason.
>
>   ARMSTRONG
>   There are ways of making a man talk,
>   Captain - get him to spill over with
>   information...Or aren't you aware of
>   that?
>
>   PARKER
>   He knew nothing of importance.
>
>   ARMSTRONG
>   Are you so sure of that? Or is it
>   just that you couldn't get it out
>   of him?

(CONTINUED)

52 CONTINUED: - 4

PARKER
I'm sure, Major, that I know how to do my job!

ARMSTRONG
Really? If it were up to me, I'd know how to make them talk!

PARKER
By beating it out of them! I know...

ARMSTRONG
Come now, Captain. A little - shall we say "persuasion" won't make any difference! It seems to me you're much too concerned with the welfare of your precious prisoners. I'm sure I could get better results!

PARKER
The same can be said for the Gestapo!

Armstrong narrows his eyes; with subdued fury.

ARMSTRONG
Look, Parker. I am the Intelligence Officer of this outfit. I expect the units, set up to supply me with information, to do their jobs. That includes you!

PARKER
Yes - sir!

ARMSTRONG
You're not dealing with children, now, Parker. This is not your language class at Buffalo High!

PARKER
I'm fully aware of that, Major. But languages was not the only thing I taught. I tried to teach my students decency along with the words!

They glare at one another. Bradford rejoins them.

BRADFORD
We'll get you your PW's, Dirk. You take it from there.

(CONTINUED)

52   CONTINUED: - 5

> PARKER
> Sir. There is one other possibility.
>
> BRADFORD
> Shoot.
>
> PARKER
> The Italian partisans, sir. If they could get us a man, who's familiar with the area over there - he might be able to get in, spot the battery, and get back to us...with some luck.
>
> BRADFORD
> It's worth a try.
>
> PARKER
> I've already requested contact.

Bradford looks questioningly at the IPW officer.

> PARKER
> So far nothing, sir.
>
> BRADFORD
> (to Armstrong;
> brusquely)
> Armstrong, I suggest you follow up Parker's request.
>
> ARMSTRONG
> Yes, sir.

He leaves.

> BRADFORD
> (his manner changes)
> Don't let Armstrong get your goat, Dirk. He's a bit rough - but he's a damned good officer.
>
> PARKER
> I'm sure he is...

Bradford starts to leave.

> BRADFORD
> We'll get you a PW - you get us the battery!

As Bradford passes the grandfather clock it suddenly starts to CHIME; it is 10:45. Bradford points to the clock.

(CONTINUED)

52 CONTINUED: - 6

> BRADFORD
> Where the hell (on earth) did that
> thing come from?

> PARKER
> Sergeant Hicks dug it out from under
> the rubble some place in the village.
> He put it in good shape. Used to be
> a watchmaker back in Jersey.

The two men look at the beautiful old clock. For a moment
the tension of war seems to be forgotten. Bradford reads
the inscription on the clock face. It is apparent from the
following conversation that a friendly relationship exists
between Bradford and his IPW.

> BRADFORD
> "Ornando Nuncio, Santa Maria."
> Might've been made right here...

> PARKER
> ...or in any one of the dozen other
> Santa Marias we've had to take.

> BRADFORD
> Always on top of some miserable,
> cold mountain...

> PARKER
> Sunny Italy...Sunny Italy, the
> travel folders used to say. I
> always thought of Italy as sunshine,
> sandy beaches, girls in bathing suits -
> and ancient ruins...Never thought I'd
> be in on making new ones myself ...
> and I never saw so many mountains!

> BRADFORD
> With the Krauts always on top of
> them - looking down our throats!
> (he grins at Parker)
> Some Intelligence expert I've got!
> Surprised about the geography of
> his battleground!

> PARKER
> (grinning back)
> I've learned, sir!

> BRADFORD
> Let's hope you'll also learn the
> location of those damned 88's!

Armstrong enters; he addresses the Colonel.

(CONTINUED)

52   CONTINUED: - 7

                    ARMSTRONG
          I've checked with Division, sir.
          They're checking Corps...

                    BRADFORD
          Confounded red tape!

He stalks from the room. Armstrong turns to Parker.

                    ARMSTRONG
          I've been thinking, Captain. If
          you find IPW work too strong for
          your belly - I might arrange a
          transfer to Special Services. You
          could run the ping-pong tournaments
          at the rest center. Think it over..!

He leaves. Parker glares after him. He is obviously
annoyed; he goes to the table. CAMERA DOLLIES IN to a
CLOSE SHOT. He sits down at the table; he picks up a pack
of cigarettes - and looks for matches; he doesn't find any;
his steel helmet is lying on the table; he lifts it up to
look under it, but there are no matches; he starts to slam
the helmet down on the table in aggravation...

53   CLOSE SHOT   U.S. ARMY STEEL HELMET

It is being slammed down on the table...

                                        MATCH CUT TO:

INT. GERMAN ARTILLERY C.P. IN CAVE   NIGHT

54   CLOSE SHOT   GERMAN WEHRMACH STEEL HELMET

It is being placed on a table. CAMERA PULLS BACK to reveal
the German C.P.

The helmet lies on a makeshift table, to which is tacked a
military area map. Major RUDOLF SCHILLER is standing at the
table; the German is in his forties, immaculately dressed,
clean shaven; he is clearing the table - pushing things aside
to get a good look at the map.

The Battery C.P. is located in a mountain cave. Efforts
have been made to make the place livable and convenient to
work in. A few shelter halves cover part of the floor;
some blankets, suspended by poles, mask the walls. A
kerosene lamp hangs from the ceiling. We see a German field
telephone and a number of small arms and other equipment.

                                        (CONTINUED)

54 CONTINUED:

Sandbags and logs have been used to reduce the size of the opening to the cave, in front of which hangs a blackout curtain. A soldier, OBERGEFREITER HANS RICHTER, is perched on a log of wood cleaning his rifle (Karabiner 98).

Schiller is studying the map before him. CAMERA DOLLIES BACK to shoot across him to the entrance of the cave, as Lt. Otto Heinrich, the Air Corps Artillery Observer, enters. He is about thirty years old and looks every inch a German. He is neat and dressed in a heavy overcoat; he carries a Schmeisser machine pistol and a pair of field glasses. (NOTE: Both officers are members of the German Aircorps, which manned the "88" batteries. They wear the appropriate uniforms.)

CAMERA PANS to include Richter, who jumps up and clicks his heels. Heinrich salutes the soldier, then he approaches Schiller and renders the Hitler salute in a rather routine manner. The relationship between the two Germans is rather formal, but not in an exaggerated way. They talk with German accents.

55 TWO SHOT   HEINRICH, SCHILLER

                  HEINRICH
        Heil Hitler! Lieutenant Heinrich
        reporting as ordered.

Schiller returns the salute.

                  SCHILLER
        Heil Hitler, Lieutenant. Make
        yourself comfortable.

                  HEINRICH
        Thank you, Herr Major.

Heinrich puts down his gear and takes off his overcoat.

                  SCHILLER
        Coffee?

                  HEINRICH
          (brightening)
        Coffee?!

                  SCHILLER
        New shipment of "Ersatz"...

Heinrich looks disappointed.

                  HEINRICH
        Yes, please.

(CONTINUED)

55   CONTINUED:

                    SCHILLER
          Warms your insides just as well.
                    (to Richter)
          Richter! Heat up some water.
          Coffee for both of us.

56   MED. SHOT   RICHTER

                    RICHTER
                    (very military)
          Jawohl, Herr Major.

Richter leaves.

57   TWO SHOT   SCHILLER, HEINRICH

Heinrich walks over to Schiller and looks down at the map.

                    SCHILLER
          Well, Lieutenant, we have a special
          fire mission coming up.

He points to a spot on the map.

                    HEINRICH
          Santa Maria?

                    SCHILLER
          Yes. We've suspected all the time
          that village might be of strategic
          importance...We were right!

                    HEINRICH
          Would be easy to level the place to
          the ground - _if_ we had the ammo.

                    SCHILLER
          We'll _have it_, Lieutenant! An
          emergency allotment is on the way.
          Three hundred rounds.

                    HEINRICH
                    (enthusiastically)
          Three hundred rounds! We can blast
          the whole place out of existence.

                    SCHILLER
          Our orders are exactly that!

Heinrich checks his eagerness and looks at Schiller questioningly.

                                        (CONTINUED)

57   CONTINUED:

> SCHILLER
> Intelligence has found out that the American Fifty Army is planning a big offensive, a push in force here - along highway 64...

> HEINRICH
> ...right through Santa Maria.

> SCHILLER
> That's the way it looks.
>   (pointing to the map)
> See that building?

58   CLOSE SHOT   HEINRICH

> HEINRICH
> The school house?

59   CLOSE SHOT   SCHILLER

> SCHILLER
> Correct. We've marked it down as a Regimental Headquarters. Remember we were scheduled to shell it last month - but didn't have the ammo?

60   TWO SHOT   SCHILLER, HEINRICH

> HEINRICH
> I remember, sir...Three rounds a day! Here we have the best guns in the world - our own eighty-eights - and no shells to fire at the enemy!

> SCHILLER
> It'll be different now.

> HEINRICH
> I certainly hope so.

> SCHILLER
> The last few days there's been more activity at the school than a regimental HQ would warrant. General officers coming and going. Place full of Signal Corps men...

> HEINRICH
> Changeover to Division HQ...?

61   MED. SHOT   SCHILLER

                    SCHILLER
          Intelligence goes even further.
          Think the place will be a Corps
          Forward CP - the hub of the
          offensive -

                    HEINRICH
                    (impressed)
          Those Intelligence boys really
          know their stuff! How did they
          manage to get that information?

                    SCHILLER
          Through one of our Fascisti friends.
          An officer of the Badoglio Division.
          Got across the lines.

                    HEINRICH
          Quite a trick!

62   MED. CLOSE SHOT   SCHILLER

                    SCHILLER
          Posed as a partisan.

63   TWO SHOT   HEINRICH, SCHILLER

                    HEINRICH
          Didn't know they had it in them...

                    SCHILLER
          Well - there are exceptions, I
          suppose. Our - "friends" - are just
          not people of military discipline.
          Just wine, women and song. Sometimes
          I wonder...
                    (he changes mood)
          This is our mission. We are to lay
          down a concentrated barrage; destroy
          every building in Santa Maria. We
          are already zeroed in on the focal
          point...
                    (he points to map)

64   MED. CLOSE SHOT   HEINRICH

                    HEINRICH
          The school.

                    SCHILLER (o.s.)
          Correct.

65   WIDER ANGLE TO ENTRANCE

Richter returns with a can of steaming coffee. He fills two canteen cups and Heinrich and Schiller take a sip. Heinrich's expression shows that the "ersatz" coffee is not to his liking; all during:

>   SCHILLER
> We'll get the guns in position after
> dark on M-Day and register on the
> target focal point.
>
>   HEINRICH
> When *is* the big show?

66   MED. CLOSE SHOT   SCHILLER

>   SCHILLER
> Day after tomorrow...at midnight
> exactly...The ammo will be here by
> then.

67   MED. CLOSE SHOT   HEINRICH

>   HEINRICH
> Day after tomorrow...
>   (with evident
>   satisfaction)
> Finally!

68   TWO SHOT   SCHILLER, HEINRICH

>   SCHILLER
>   (referring to map)
> I want *you* to establish an
> Observation Post there - on Monte
> Adone.
>
>   HEINRICH
> Good spot. I've directed fire from
> there before. There is a small farm
> house. Very suitable.
>
>   SCHILLER
> I want you to be in position tomorrow
> night - a full 24 hours before M-Hour.
>
>   HEINRICH
> Yes, sir.
>
>   SCHILLER
> I want reports on all activity in
> Santa Maria during the period
> immediately preceding the mission.

(CONTINUED)

68   CONTINUED:

                    HEINRICH
          I understand.

                    SCHILLER
          Sergeant Mueller will establish a
          second OP...
                    (pointing)
          ...seven kilometers to the West of
          you - to assure success of the
          mission - just in case...

                    HEINRICH
          Very good. What's the communications
          set-up?

                    SCHILLER
          The wire crews are already at work.
          How long will it take you to get
          up there?

                    HEINRICH
          It's a good three hours' climb.

                    SCHILLER
          Take two men with you - one on the
          field phone.

                    HEINRICH
          I'll take Richter - and Corporal
          Krim.

Heinrich prepares to leave; he puts on his overcoat and
picks up his gear, during:

                    SCHILLER
          Everything clear?

                    HEINRICH
          Yes, sir.

                    SCHILLER
          Good.

Schiller sits down on an improvised seat. The official
business out of the way his manner of speaking assumes a
less formal tone.

                    SCHILLER
          Any news from Hilda?

                    HEINRICH
          Not for a while, sir. I only hope
          she left Dresden before the heavy
          raids.

                                        (CONTINUED)

68   CONTINUED: - 2

                    SCHILLER
          I'm sure she did. She's a clever
          girl that wife of yours.

                    HEINRICH
          Thank you.

                    SCHILLER
          Don't believe every rumor you hear,
          Otto. Those reports of heavy
          damage at home are greatly exaggerated.

                    HEINRICH
                (he is not
                 convinced)
          I suppose so, sir.

                    SCHILLER
          Things'll be better soon. I have
          it from way up that the Fuehrer has
          promised us a new secret weapon.

69   MED. CLOSE SHOT   HEINRICH

      He shows some doubt in the statement.

                    HEINRICH
          If the Fuehrer has a secret weapon,
          now's the time to use it.

70   MED. CLOSE SHOT   SCHILLER

                    SCHILLER
                (sharply)
          The Fuehrer will use it, when he
          sees fit!

71   CLOSE SHOT   HEINRICH

      He is about to say something, but thinks better of it.
      Obviously he does not have the same faith in the Fuehrer's
      promises as does his superior.

72   CLOSE SHOT   SCHILLER

                    SCHILLER
                (sternly)
          That's all, Lieutenant!

73   MED. TWO SHOT   HEINRICH, SCHILLER

> HEINRICH
> (formally)
> Yes, sir. With your permission,
> Herr Major, I shall be on my way.
>
> SCHILLER
> (informal again)
> Alright, Otto..."Hals-und-Beinbruch!"
> And let's have some real fireworks!
>
> HEINRICH
> The Coventry treatment, sir. Santa
> Maria will be wiped out! Heil Hitler!
>
> SCHILLER
> Heil Hitler!

CAMERA DOLLIES BACK as Heinrich walks toward the exit. Richter again jumps up from his log, clicking his heels and saluting the departing Heinrich.

74   CLOSE SHOT   SCHILLER

He looks after Heinrich with a thoughtful expression; then he sighs. He "hunts" for a cigarette; finds a half-empty pack in his pocket. He pulls out a cigarette - and looks at it without any real pleasure; then he gives a little shrug of resignation - much as if to say, "Ah, well, an 'ersatz' cigarette is still better than no cigarette at all!" He lights the cigarette and takes a deep puff. Obviously, he does not enjoy the taste...With a small gesture of annoyance he brings down the cigarette to stub it out in a can lid on the table...

MATCH CUT TO:

INT. IPW ROOM OF SANTA MARIA SCHOOL HOUSE   NIGHT

75   CLOSE SHOT   RATION CAN LID ON TABLE

A hand comes INTO THE SHOT and stubs out a cigarette butt. CAMERA PULLS OUT to a MED. CLOSE SHOT of Parker. He is seated at his desk; he is stubbing out his cigarette in the can lid. He gets up, stretches - and glances at the grandfather clock.

76   CLOSE SHOT   GRANDFATHER CLOCK

It shows 11:07.

77   MED. SHOT

   Parker leaves the room.

EXT. SANTA MARIA SCHOOL HOUSE   NIGHT

78   MED. WIDE SHOT

   Parker comes out of the school house. He walks towards the village square.

EXT. SANTA MARIA VILLAGE SQUARE   NIGHT

79   MED. SHOT   PARKER   PAN SHOT

   Parker crosses the square. He walks into one of the streets going off the square.

EXT. SANTA MARIA STREET   NIGHT

80   MED. GROUP SHOT   THREE SOLDIERS ("ROMEO," SAM, PINTO) HICKS, ALVIN

   They are sitting around the broken railing of the front porch of a little house shooting the breeze. They're passing around a photo of a girl. Alvin is looking at it.

               ALVIN
      Got yourself quite a wife, there,
      boy...ni-i-i-ce..!

               HICKS
      Never figured you for a family
      man, Sam. Why'd you get hitched?

               SAM
            (drily)
      To beat the draft!

               HICKS
      Clever - cle-ver!

               ROMEO
      Me - I'll never get hooked. I'll
      stick to being best man.

               HICKS
      Just one thing wrong with being
      best man at somebody's wedding, Romeo...

               ROMEO
      Yeah? What's that?

                              (CONTINUED)

80 CONTINUED:

>   HICKS
> You never get a chance to prove it!

The men laugh and groan in protest.

>   ALVIN
> I dunno...Marriage is okay. Once
> had an uncle, who wanted to get
> married real bad. Advertised for a
> wife in the paper. He got more'n
> three hundred replies...'Course most
> of 'em said the same thing...

>   PINTO
> Yeah? What?

>   ALVIN
> Just - "You can have mine!"

The men laugh.

81 WIDER ANGLE

Parker is seen approaching on the street and passing the group; he is caught up in his own thoughts - oblivious to the group of G.I.'s ...Hicks spots him.

>   HICKS
> Evening, Captain.

Parker makes no reply; he walks on - deep in thought.

82 CLOSE SHOT   HICKS

He looks after Parker with a little frown.

83 GROUP SHOT

PINTO, a frail little fellow, slaps an insect on his neck.

>   PINTO
> Arrhh - those buggers! They're
> man-eaters!

>   ROMEO
> Then you got nothing to worry about!

>   ALVIN
> Why - they don't hardly mean
> anything...I remember back in
> Louisiana on maneuvers. We had
> mosquitos.
>   (MORE)

(CONTINUED)

83   CONTINUED:

                        ALVIN (CONT'D)
              Now there was big buggers. Man -
              were they huge - and choosy!? Why -
              they use'ta come in at night and turn
              your dogtag over to see what your
              bloodtype was!

    The men laugh and kid....

EXT. SANTA MARIA STREET   NIGHT

84   SHOT

    Parker is slowly walking through the dark street; he is
    serious and thoughtful; there is no one abroad; he passes a
    small house - hardly more than a hut; a handpainted sign
    on it proclaims:

                    O F F I C E R S   C L U B

                    Rooms with adjoining towels

EXT. EDGE OF SANTA MARIA VILLAGE   NIGHT

85   LONG SHOT

    The place seems deserted; Parker walks on to the scene; he
    goes to an overturned wagon and leans against it.

86   CLOSER ANGLE

    Parker is leaning against the wagon; he looks toward the
    mountains - the battlefields in the far distance...

87   EXTREME LONG SHOT   MOUNTAINS   POV   PARKER (STOCK)

    In the far distance faint, occasional flashes of artillery
    fire can be seen over the mountains - followed by a low,
    ominous rumble.

88   CLOSE SHOT   PARKER

    He sighs; he looks grim...Suddenly a small noise comes from
    the darkness of one of the ruined farm houses. Parker at
    once stiffens. He gets an expression of alertness on his
    face; he listens intently...He strains to see.

89   LONG SHOT   RUINED FARM HOUSE   POV   PARKER

The broken, crumbled ruins look dark and forbidding with shadows of stygian darkness. But there is no movement to be seen.

90   MED. CLOSEUP   PARKER

He is looking toward the ruins; all is silent - he begins to relax, when - from the other side - the low rattle of small stones makes him freeze...and from his right, his left, all in front of him come little furtive night noises... Slowly Parker draws his '45, holding it at the ready.

                PARKER
              (low, tensely)
    Who goes there?

There is no answer.

91   SHOT   ACROSS PARKER TO RUINS

All is quiet...Then again the tell-tale rattle of debris... and suddenly a dark figure appears from out of the black shadows to loom ominously, silently in front of Parker... And even as Parker raises his gun to firing position several other figures rise up out of the darkness like black apparitions...Quietly Parker looks around; he seems to be surrounded by silent, shadowy figures...

92   CLOSE SHOT   PARKER

He looks grim - tensely alert.

93   MED. SHOT

Immobile the quiet, dark figures stand facing the lone man - then one of them steps into the moonlight.

94   CLOSER SHOT   MAN

He is a huge, fierce looking man clad in a comglomeration of insignialess Italian and German uniform pieces and civilian clothes; a black stubble beard covers his strong chin, and in his hands he carelessly holds a German Schmeisser machine pistol. Gruffly he says:

                MAN
    I am Volpe - the Fox!

95   MED. SHOT

   Volpe slowly walks up to Parker; the other figures close in, but keep some little distance.

96   TWO SHOT   VOLPE, PARKER

   They look at one another; then Volpe breaks into a grin. He nods meaningfully towards the German lines with his huge head.

                    VOLPE
         Over there - in the dark, it would
         not be healthy for an officer - alone!

                    PARKER
               (he has regained
                his composure)
         You are the partisans...the Italian
         Partisans?

                    VOLPE
         Yes.

                    PARKER
         I am Captain Parker...

                    VOLPE
         I know.

                    PARKER
         I asked them to send you here.

                    VOLPE
         Yes. We talk now. You take us.

                    PARKER
         Come on.

97   MED. SHOT

   Parker starts away, followed by Volpe. Volpe motions to two of his band to come along, to the rest he snaps:

                    VOLPE
         Resta!

   Then he, Parker and the two partisans walk back into the village.

98   MED. SHOT   ANOTHER ANGLE   SAME LOCATION

   The four are passing close by a low, crumbled wall - when a figure steps out of the shadows.

(CONTINUED)

98   CONTINUED:

It is a G.I. - it is Hicks! In his hands he has a Thompson sub-machine gun. He grins at Parker and Volpe.

                   HICKS
Thought we'd play too, Captain!
Hope you don't mind.
         (he turns and calls)
Okay, you guys, get lost! This is a private party!

99   WIDE SHOT

Out of the dark ruins four more figures rise, the men with whom we saw Hicks earlier...Grinning they watch Parker and the partisans, as they walk towards the school house...

100   CLOSE SHOT   HICKS

He is looking after them. He leans back against the cracked wall, and grimaces as something jabs him in the back; he reaches behind him and pulls forth a long piece of twisted iron; it is impossible to tell, what it once was; Hicks looks at it, shrugs and hurls it at the ground as one would a knife...

                           MATCH CUT TO:

<u>INT. IPW ROOM OF SANTA MARIA SCHOOL HOUSE   NIGHT</u>

101   CLOSE SHOT   KNIFE

It is hurtling down, burying its sharp tip in the floor to stand quivering from the force...

102   MED. SHOT

Volpe is sitting in Parker's chair; he has evidently just used his long, wicked looking knife to slice open a K-ration before hurling it at the floor; now - and during the following - he is happily exploring the K-ration contents, treating the cigarettes, he finds, as special treasures. In the b.g. - huddled next to the pot bellied stove for warmth - sit the two other partisans, their backs to Parker and Volpe - and CAMERA. Hicks is at the door.

                   VOLPE
It is not possible what you ask.
For weeks now the Germans have
closed up the area - very tight...
so -

                             (CONTINUED)

102   CONTINUED:

He **squeezes** the empty K-ration box flat in one of his huge hands.

                PARKER
          Then you can't penetrate their
          security?

Volpe - chewing a fruit bar with evident relish - shakes his head.

                PARKER
         And the 88's?

Volpe shrugs.

                VOLPE
         They are there...but where?

He shrugs again. Parker looks disappointed.

                VOLPE
         The people behind the German lines -
         they are not permitted to leave their
         farms - their villages..."Verboten!"
         With them what is not compulsory is
         forbidden!

He spits contemptuously on the floor; then he looks up at Parker with a shrewd look.

                VOLPE
             (continues)
         It is not possible for us to go
         look for your guns...But one person
         - one, who will not stick out like
         a corn stalk in a wheat field - one,
         who knows the people and the places
         over there - such a one would perhaps
         have luck...

                PARKER
         That's what I've been looking for!

                VOLPE
         I brought you! One of us - born
         just across - in Soncino...One supposes
         someone that knows the area well!

                PARKER
         Where is he?

                VOLPE
             (grins; he nods
             towards the stove)
         There. By the stove. The little one!

Parker quickly looks.

103   MED. WIDE SHOT   STOVE   POV PARKER

The two partisans, their backs to Parker, sit warming themselves at the stove. One of them displays a broad, hefty back - the other is slight and small - almost frail looking.

104   TWO SHOT   PARKER, VOLPE

Parker looks back at Volpe with a small frown.

> PARKER
> (low voice)
> That little guy!? What makes you think he can handle a job like this?

> VOLPE
> (with a mirthless grin)
> My people know how to take care of themselves. All of them..

He pulls his big knife from the floor and holds it out towards Parker.

> VOLPE
> (in a hoarse whisper)
> Try. Take him - by surprise!

105   CLOSEUP   PARKER

Startled at the unexpected turn of events Parker hesitates.

106   CLOSEUP   VOLPE

A look of contemptuous scorn begins to creep into the partisan leader's eyes.

107   TWO SHOT   PARKER, VOLPE

Parker takes the knife. He studies Volpe for a moment. These are rough people, he's dealing with. Death to them is commonplace - personal safety hardly worth the consideration...But courage - or the lack of it - is! And Parker needs the partisans; he cannot afford to lose their respect.

Slowly, silently he gets up; balancing the huge knife in his right hand he noiselessly starts to move up behind the unsuspecting youngster...

108 CLOSE SHOT   VOLPE

He is watching with keen interest.

109 MED. SHOT

Parker reaches a position directly behind the young partisan. He places the razor-sharp knife point an inch from the partisan's back - then, as he suddenly presses it lightly into the loose-fitting jacket, he orders:

> PARKER
> Don't move!

Instantly the young partisan explodes into action; in one movement he ducks away from the pressure of the knife, leaps to his feet, whirls on Parker...his left hand is brought back and down in a numbing blow, which catapults Parker's knife arm to the side, nearly making him lose his grip on his weapon with its sudden force and violence; in the partisan's right hand there suddenly gleams the murderous steel of a German bayonet, honed to razor sharpness; the partisan's cap flies off with the vehemence of the motion - and the two of them are facing each other - arms held out in front, slightly apart, each with a wicked knife point aimed directly at the other!

110 CLOSE SHOT   PARKER

He stands rooted to the spot - incredulity on his shocked face, as he stares in astonishment at his mock opponent ...

111 CLOSE SHOT   PARTISAN

In the violence of the action the partisan's cap has flown off - the loose fitting coat fallen open. Huge, dark eyes flash angrily at Parker from a lovely face, framed by unruly, close-cut black hair; full red lips are slightly parted in excitement - and the open coat leaves no doubts that Parker is facing a beautiful, young girl! Volpe comes up to the two of them; he wears a huge grin.

> VOLPE
> (to Parker)
> Her name is Rina.
> (to Rina)
> He is the American who wants you.
>
> RINA
> He is a fool! If he had been a Nazi - he would be dead now!

She puts away her knife; with a contemptuous look at Parker she turns her back on him and again sits down near the stove.

112 TWO SHOT   VOLPE, PARKER

> PARKER
> (annoyed)
> A girl! You expect me to use her as an infiltration agent? That's no kid's stuff!...A girl!...

> VOLPE
> A girl - yes. But not just <u>any</u> girl! You found out! Rina is like a she-panther. She has killed...
> (he holds up
> his fingers)
> ...seven Nazis!

> PARKER
> But - I can't send a girl behind enemy lines.

Volpe shrugs.

> VOLPE
> I can. They will question her less - than a man, who should be fighting...

> PARKER
> (he shakes his head)
> No go, Volpe.

Volpe turns to Rina.

> VOLPE
> Rina...

113 WIDER ANGLE

The girl joins the two men.

> VOLPE
> The American does not wish that you go across - to Soncino.

> RINA
> (at once defiant)
> Why?!

> VOLPE
> He does not like you are a girl!

Rina's eyes flash at Parker; she looks him up and down.

> RINA
> I already say - he is a fool!

(CONTINUED)

113 CONTINUED:

                    PARKER
Now look here...

                    RINA
               (flaring up)
I do not need you to like me to go
across. I go anyway!

                    PARKER
You don't - if I keep you here!

                    RINA
You stop me?

                    PARKER
I can't send you ...

                    RINA
I go! If you wish I look for
special things - you better tell
me.

Parker glares at the defiant girl. He turns to Volpe.

                    PARKER
Wait outside.

Volpe leaves with Rina and Tony. Hicks comes up to Parker.

                    HICKS
Quite a show, Captain!

                    PARKER
I felt like a damned fool. But
I had to go through with it.
They're a rough bunch. I thought
I'd better play their game.

                    HICKS
Are you going to let the girl
try to get across?

                    PARKER
I don't know. The final decision
is up to Colonel Bradford.

<u>INT. S-2 ROOM IN SANTA MARIA SCHOOL HOUSE</u>   NIGHT

114 CLOSE SHOT BRADFORD   DOLLY OUT TO GROUP SHOT

                    BRADFORD
               (frowning)
...We can't be choosy, Dirk. We
need that damned information. If
the girl is willing to go...

                              (CONTINUED)

114   CONTINUED:

CAMERA REVEALS Rina and Parker.

     RINA
    (firmly)
 I go.

     BRADFORD
 Alright. We'll take a chance on you.

CAMERA REVEALS Armstrong and Volpe.

     ARMSTRONG
 It's too late to send her out
 tonight - thanks to Parker -

     BRADFORD
 I hate like hell to lose more
 time...

115 TWO SHOT RINA, BRADFORD

     RINA
 It is urgent - this information you
 want?

     BRADFORD
 More than you can realize.

     RINA
 Then I go - tonight - now!

Bradford looks at the girl speculatively; she returns his gaze firmly.

     BRADFORD
 Alright!

He turns to Parker.

116 GROUP SHOT

     BRADFORD
 Dirk, brief her. Make sure she
 knows exactly what we want.

     PARKER
 Yes, sir.

<u>INT. IPW ROOM IN SANTA MARIA SCHOOL HOUSE NIGHT</u>

117 CLOSE SHOT AREA MAP

Parker's hand comes INTO FRAME and indicates the area around the village of Soncino.

         (CONTINUED)

117   CONTINUED:

>   PARKER (o.s.)
>   Somewhere in this area...As you can
>   see, somewhere around Soncino.

118   TWO SHOT   PARKER   RINA

They are studying the map on Parker's table.

>   RINA
>   There are many places there, that
>   such guns you speak of could be
>   hidden.

>   PARKER
>   You'll have to find the one place
>   they <u>are</u> using.

Rina straightens up; she has removed her loose fitting coat - and the masculine cut of the tight khaki shirt, she is wearing, only accentuates her soft femininity. She begins to get herself ready for her patrol; she inspects her knife; she slips into a warm, tightfitting sweater - and hides her hair under a cap, during:

>   RINA
>   If I can get through - I find out.
>   There are many patrols....many
>   checks...everything very strict...

Parker looks at the girl; he is obviously impressed by her wild, young beauty.

>   PARKER
>   Rina. Look - it's a dangerous job.
>   Don't you think...

>   RINA
>   (interrupting)
>   It is also a much important job.
>   It must be done. I do it!

She looks at Parker, coldly and defiantly sullen. Her natural feminine softness and warmth, which we feel is there beneath her cold exterior, seem to be encased in a shell of hard determination. Her mind seems to run unwaveringly in one direction...fight, kill the Fascists and the Nazis..! Parker again refers to the map; Rina joins him at the table.

>   PARKER
>   There's only one place you can
>   even hope to get through the
>   mountains...This sector...here...

(CONTINUED)

118   CONTINUED:

>   RINA
>   I know.
>
>   PARKER
>   It's well guarded...Patrols all over
>   the place...
>
>   RINA
>   If anybody <u>can</u> get through - I can!
>   Someone <u>try</u> to stop me...I know how
>   to kill!

Parker looks at the girl; after a pause he says soberly:

>   PARKER
>   Alright, Rina...Any questions?
>
>   RINA
>   No...I am ready.
>
>   PARKER
>   I'll take you to the line...

They leave. CAMERA DOLLIES IN ON THE MAP to a CLOSE SHOT of the area around Soncino village behind the German lines...

<u>EXT. ROCKY HILLSIDE FIELD AND BRUSH AREA   NIGHT</u>

119   WIDE SHOT

It is a hillside area, part fields, part shrubbery...All is quiet - then a shadowy figure can be seen briefly moving down the slope, L to R, into hiding behind a bush.

120   CLOSE SHOT   RINA

Like a silent wraith the girl steals through the brush.

121   ANOTHER ANGLE   WIDER SHOT

The girl silently, cautiously - yet with amazing speed - makes her way towards the German lines...

122   CLOSE SHOT

Rina crawls to a vantage point; she looks down the slope intently.

123 LONG SHOT   POV   RINA

Across the entire area in front of her a couple of rows of accordion type barbed wire are strung irregularly.

124 MED. SHOT   RINA

She makes her way off to the right.

125 ANOTHER ANGLE   MED. SHOT

Rina comes to an open field; there is a sign on a low post; she looks at it.

126 CLOSEUP   SIGN

It has a skull and crossbones on it; it reads:

ACHTUNG MINEN!

127 CLOSE SHOT   RINA

She crawls off.

128 ANOTHER ANGLE   MED. SHOT

Rina is carefully making her way through the brush and rocks; she stops in a place of cover...

129 CLOSE SHOT   RINA

Again she looks intently ahead...

130 LONG SHOT   POV   RINA

The accordion barbed wire is still in front of her - but closer; we can see several tin cans hanging from the strands...As the girl is watching a small group of German soldiers on horseback slowly rides patrol on the other side of the wire.

131 MED. SHOT   RINA

Cautiously she crawls off to the left...

132 ANOTHER ANGLE   MED. SHOT

Rina is inching her way into a position of cover; she looks ahead again.

133 LONG SHOT   POV   RINA

Ahead is the barbed wire; there is no movement to be seen.

134 MED. SHOT   RINA

She begins to move towards the wire...Suddenly there is the startling sound of something leaping up and crashing through the shrubs. Instantly Rina flattens herself on the ground.

135 WIDER ANGLE

A startled deer is running from the shrubs from a spot near Rina's place of concealment.

136 CLOSE SHOT   RINA

Cautiously she looks up.

137 LONG SHOT   POV   RINA

The startled deer is running directly at the barbed wire; it leaps at it; the cans begin to rattle loudly...At once a flare explodes into the air - brilliantly illuminating the area - and almost simultaneously two light machine guns from different emplacements open up...The deer runs away in panic!

138 CLOSE SHOT   RINA

Grimly she has watched the incident; she starts away - out of frame.

139 ANOTHER LOCATION   MED. SHOT

Rina is taking cover behind a rock; she cautiously looks out.

140 LONG SHOT   POV   RINA

At the bottom of a small dirt road a little bridge runs across a small stream; there is a small hut on the far side...A lone German soldier is standing guard.

141 MED. CLOSE SHOT   RINA

She looks grim; she takes out her knife - and slowly, quietly she crawls from the hiding place towards the bridge...

142 MED. SHOT   GERMAN SENTRY

He is completely at ease - leaning against the bridge railing.

143 CLOSE SHOT   RINA

Quietly she is making her way towards the bridge...She stops and looks.

144 SHOT POV   RINA

The bridge is quite near; the sentry is standing with his back to the girl.

145 CLOSE SHOT   RINA

With a burning, fanatic hate illuminating her huge eyes she looks at the sentry; then she looks at the gleaming knife in her hand - and she is just about to leave her cover for the bridge - when several voices suddenly are HEARD from the bridge...Startled she looks.

146 SHOT   POV   RINA

Down on the bridge the sentry is being joined by three other men; they ad lib jokingly in German.

147 CLOSE SHOT   RINA

She looks furiously frustrated. With a gesture of annoyance she puts her knife away...and starts back.

148 ANOTHER LOCATION   MED. SHOT

Rina is returning to the American lines; she moves fast - but silently...travelling R to L.

EXT. WOODED HIGH GROUND OF MONTE ADONE   NIGHT

149 MED. SHOT

Rina - moving R to L - is on her way back.

150 CLOSE SHOT   RINA

She stops, listens - then moves on.

151 MED. SHOT   RINA

She is coming to an area of shrubbery on the sparsely wooded slope; suddenly she stops dead in her tracks...In the distance can be HEARD the faint sounds of many footsteps approaching. Instantly the girl takes cover.

152 CLOSE SHOT   RINA

She tries to draw herself further in under the bush - but she suddenly discovers that her foot is entangled in a wire running along the ground...The SOUND of the footsteps comes closer...Rina freezes - her leg sticking out from under the bush.

153 WIDER ANGLE

A German patrol - returning from a reconnaisance mission, going R to L - passes by within feet of Rina's hiding place.

154 SHOT POV RINA

Lying under the bush - one foot sticking out into the open - she sees the hobnailed boots of the patrol members tramp by, literally almost stepping on her foot!

155 WIDE SHOT

The German soldiers disappear into the woods - unaware of Rina.

156 CLOSE SHOT RINA

Cautiously she begins to try and free herself from the entanglement of the wire; it proves difficult; she pulls her knife and is just about to cut the wire - when she suddenly stops; she holds up the wire and looks closely at it.

157 CLOSEUP   WIRE IN RINA'S HAND

She is holding it - fingering it in examination.

                                                  MATCH CUT TO:

<u>INT. IPW ROOM IN SANTA MARIA SCHOOL HOUSE   NIGHT</u>

158 CLOSEUP   PENCIL IN PARKER'S HAND

He is fingering it - then he lets it drop on the desk.

                                                  (CONTINUED)

158   CONTINUED:

>   PARKER (o.s.)
>   Then - there was no way for you to
>   get through.

159   TWO SHOT   RINA, PARKER

Parker is seated at his desk; Rina is standing in front of it - still clad in her patrol outfit.

>   RINA
>   (belligerently)
>   You are thinking - if I had been a
>   man - I would have gone through!
>   You are wrong!
>
>   PARKER
>   I'm glad you didn't take any foolish
>   chances, Rina...

He gets up.

160   WIDER ANGLE

Hicks and Volpe stand silently to one side; they look as disappointed and dejected as Parker himself. Parker goes to the window and draws the blackout curtains aside; outside the gray light of dawn can be seen; then he turns back to Rina; all during:

>   RINA
>   Better I get back and tell you this -
>   than I get caught! Then you send
>   someone else to get caught! You must
>   get your information some other way.
>   Nobody get through German lines now..!
>
>   PARKER
>   Thank you for trying, Rina...
>
>   RINA
>   Maybe I do more for you than try...
>   (she grabs the wire
>   from the field
>   telephone)
>   Look! On the slope of Monte Adone -
>   high up - I find a wire...
>   (she holds up the
>   phone wire)
>   .... like this!

Parker strides to her; he takes the wire from her.

161 CLOSEUP PARKER

With an excited, questioning expression on his face he looks at Rina.

>   RINA (o.s.)
>   Yes...Just like that!

Parker looks at the wire in his hand.

162 CLOSEUP WIRE IN PARKER'S HAND

It is the typical twisted wire of a communications line!

MATCH CUT TO:

EXT. SANTA MARIA SCHOOL YARD   MORNING

163 CLOSE SHOT BUNCH OF WIRES

They are coming out of a window in the school - along with a sooty stove pipe...CAMERA PANS ALONG the wires to a MED. SHOT of Colonel Bradford. He is stripped to the waist except for his O.D. undershirt; a couple of school desks have been brought out into the yard; on one of them stand the inevitable up-turned steel helmet - and a canteen; on a line strung from the building hang several items of O.D. laundry...Bradford is in the process of brushing his teeth from his canteen cup.

164 ANOTHER ANGLE

Armstrong and Parker enter the school yard and walk up to Bradford.

>   ARMSTRONG
>   Sorry to bother you, sir. But
>   Captain Parker insists on seeing you.
>
>   BRADFORD
>   (brushing his teeth)
>   'ot a'out?
>
>   ARMSTRONG
>   Some hare-brained idea...
>
>   PARKER
>   (firmly)
>   Sir, I'd like permission to go on
>   tonight's combat patrol.

Bradford rinses his mouth and spits the water on the ground.

(CONTINUED)

164   CONTINUED:

                    BRADFORD
          Out of the question!

                    ARMSTRONG
          I already told him that, sir.

                    BRADFORD
          I can't afford to send you on patrol.

                    PARKER
          Sir, this is a special case.

                    BRADFORD
          No, Dirk!

                    PARKER
          ...I have a very valid reason.

Bradford looks at him.

                    BRADFORD
          Alright. Let's hear it.

                    ARMSTRONG
                  (protesting)
          Sir...

                    BRADFORD
                  (cutting him off)
          I want to hear the Captain's reason,
          Major.

                    PARKER
          The partisan girl, sir, the one
          who tried to cross the line. She
          ran into a German communication wire
          on Monte Adone. A communication
          wire, sir! It could very well be
          live. An O.P. line to the battery,
          we're looking for!

                    BRADFORD
          Go on.

                    PARKER
          You know I speak German fluently,
          sir. If I could locate that wire -
          I might easily pick up a clue to
          the battery position, by listening
          in!

Bradford thinks it over.

                    BRADFORD
          Might work at that...Alright, Dirk.
          Go along.

                                        (CONTINUED)

164 CONTINUED: - 2

>   PARKER
>   Thank you, sir!
>
>   BRADFORD
>   Just don't get yourself captured!

Bradford picks up his helmet and pours the water in it out on the ground.

165 CLOSE SHOT   WATER

It is splashing on the ground...

                              MATCH CUT TO:

EXT. SANTA MARIA VILLAGE SQUARE   DAY

166 CLOSE SHOT   WATER IN FOUNTAIN

It is splashing in the fountain.

167 WIDE SHOT   FOUNTAIN

A bunch of G.I.'s are hanging around the fountain; we recognize Pinto, Sam, Hicks and Alvin with Luigi in tow. There is general ad lib conversation and bantering; the men seem to be in high spirits...Romeo comes hurrying on to the scene; he looks as spic and span as possible under the circumstances; he has polished his boots and is finishing tying a tie! He runs up to Hicks.

>   ROMEO
>   Hey! What's the scoop? Did it
>   come yet?

Hicks makes a great and earnest to do about looking around; then -

>   HICKS
>   D'you see it?
>
>   ROMEO
>   No!
>
>   HICKS
>   There's your answer.

Romeo walks over to a group of G.I.'s sitting around at the base of the fountain; Sam, Pinto and Alvin...

168 FOUR SHOT

Romeo joins the three G.I.'s; he makes himself comfortable.

>   ROMEO
>   Ahhhh! La bella Italy! Where wine
>   and women grow on trees!

>   ALVIN
>   I'll take the good old U.S. victory
>   garden variety...

He looks o.s.

169 LONG SHOT   POV ALVIN

A very heavy Italian woman walks by with a basket under one arm and pulling a small child with the other.

170 FOUR SHOT

>   SAM
>   It's great country, men...if you
>   didn't have to fight your way
>   through it!

>   PINTO
>   You kidding? Hills - hills - hills...
>   up an' down - up an' down ... My
>   feet are killing me!

>   SAM
>   (expansively)
>   Those hills are a fisherman's
>   paradise, my boy. In season those
>   mountain streams up there oughta
>   be full of trout.
>   (to Alvin)
>   Ever do any fishing, Alvin?

>   ALVIN
>   Yeah. But I don't like to brag
>   about it.

>   ROMEO
>   Here it comes!

>   PINTO
>   What d'ya mean, brag?

>   ALVIN
>   Well - back home we had this here
>   creek. Fissinger's Creek we called
>   it. Had the biggest trout you ever
>   saw.

(CONTINUED)

170   CONTINUED:

> PINTO
> Ever catch yourself a winner?

> ALVIN
> Sure did. I oncet caught a whopper.
> Had a picture taken of it.

> PINTO
> A real big one, eh?

> ALVIN
> Big? Why, it was so big even the
> photograph weighed three pounds!

With an outraged howl the others start to pummel him.

171   ANOTHER ANGLE

Hicks jumps to his feet.

> HICKS
> Here she comes!

172   LONG SHOT   POV   HICKS

Chugging into the square comes a Red Cross Clubmobile.

173   WIDE SHOT

The Clubmobile drives onto the square and stops; the G.I.'s all cluster around it in loud excitement...

174   CLOSER ANGLE   FEATURING TRUCK CAB DOOR

Several G.I.'s are gathered around the door in anticipation. Romeo pulls out his OD handkerchief; with a flourish he dusts off the running board - and then spreads out the cloth on the ground like a latter-day Sir Walter Raleigh...The cab door opens - and an expectant hush falls over the men... And then a Red Cross Girl, SUSIE, a well-endowed, cheery blonde, steps out...The men as one give a deep sigh - before bedlam breaks loose - as they all crowd around Susie.

175   TWO SHOT   HICKS, ALVIN

> HICKS
> (impressed)
> Wow! Is she stacked!

(CONTINUED)

175 CONTINUED:

> ALVIN
> Man! She's built like a brick shower stall!

176 GROUP SHOT

The G.I.'s are crowded around the Clubmobile; there is general high-spirited hubbub and ad libbing. Susie opens the wagon.

> SUSIE
> Come and get it!

177 CLOSE SHOT   ROMEO

> ROMEO
> (eagerly)
> That's for me! Wow! A real piece of art!

178 MED. SHOT   SUSIE (G.I.'S)

> SUSIE
> Coffee, doughnuts, cake...On the house!

179 CLOSE SHOT   ROMEO

> ROMEO
> (mock disappointment)
> Oh, *that!*...Ah, well...
>   (he prances towards
>   the truck)
> Cigars, cigarettes...lipstick!

180 GROUP SHOT

Around the front of the Clubmobile comes another Red Cross Girl, JOANIE, a pretty brunette; she is followed by Sam, who carries a phonograph; he places it on the hood of the truck - and soon the music of a jitterbug band blares forth.

181 INTERCUTS AS NEEDED

It is a scene of happy merry-making and clowning -- Time off from the grim business of war...The soldiers enjoy the refreshments; they dance with the girls - generally hamming it up.

182   CLOSER ANGLE   MED. SHOT

Romeo is doing some fancy stepping with Susie; suddenly he finds himself apparently with Hicks as a partner; with exaggerated horror he pulls away; Hicks grins and turns to Sam.

                    HICKS
The story of my life. Even at school everybody hated me because I was too popular!

183   WIDE SHOT   DOLLY IN

CAMERA SLOWLY DOLLIES IN through the milling, shouting, laughing crowd towards the Clubmobile; towards the truck cab; towards the door to a CLOSE SHOT of the door. On it is the Red Cross Emblem...

                    MATCH CUT TO:

INT. HEINRICH'S BUNKER   NIGHT

184   CLOSE SHOT   BOX LID WITH RED CROSS

It is standing open; on it is a large Red Cross...The lid is closed as CAMERA PULLS BACK revealing Cpl. Krim, Richter and Lt. Heinrich; they are getting ready to set out for the O.P. Richter has just taken out a couple of bandage packs from the medical chest; he gives one to Heinrich and keeps one himself.

185   CLOSER ANGLE

Heinrich is looking over his binoculars; Krim is checking his rifle.

                    HEINRICH
                 (to Krim)
Corporal, take along enough extra clips.

                    KRIM
Jawohl, Herr Lieutenant.

                    HEINRICH
The wire crew didn't run into anything up there...but we'll play it safe.

Heinrich reaches for his belt.

                          (CONTINUED)

185   CONTINUED:

> HEINRICH
> It won't be long now, boys. You'll have a grandstand view of some real pretty fireworks!

The men grin.

186   CLOSE SHOT   HEINRICH

He buckles on his belt; the black-holstered Luger pistol dangles heavily from his hip. Heinrich reaches to adjust it.

187   CLOSEUP   LUGER

Heinrich's hand is adjusting it in its holster...

MATCH CUT TO:

INT. IPW ROOM OF SANTA MARIA SCHOOL HOUSE   NIGHT

188   CLOSEUP   U.S. ARMY '45

It is being adjusted in its holster.

189   MED. CLOSE SHOT   PARKER

He is adjusting the '45 hanging from his webbed belt; he is getting ready to go on the combat patrol. CAMERA WIDENS to reveal Hicks. The Sergeant is helping Parker getting ready. Parker takes his I.D. papers and personal belongings from his pockets and hands them to Hicks, during:

> PARKER
> (with a sort of gallows-humor)
> So - what'll you have? An officer? Noncom? Infantry? Artillery? Panzer? Any particular unit number?

> HICKS
> Well - since you ask. How about a nice German Wac - about nineteen... 36 - 23 - 36?

Parker grins; he hands his belongings to Hicks.

> PARKER
> Here - that makes me clean. Hang on to them for me.

(CONTINUED)

189   CONTINUED:

>   HICKS
>   Sure thing.

Parker is ready; he nods towards the grandfather clock.

>   PARKER
>   That museum piece of yours keep
>   time?
>
>   HICKS
>   Right on the button.

Parker looks at the clock.

190   CLOSE SHOT   GRANDFATHER CLOCK

It shows 10:37.

                                        MATCH CUT TO:

EXT. AMERICAN FRONT LINE POSITION   NIGHT

191   CLOSE SHOT   WATCH

It shows 11:00 sharp.

192   WIDER ANGLE

The watch is on the wrist of SGT. DAVIS, the patrol leader, who's looking at it; he and Parker along with the rest of the patrol are waiting near a machine gun emplacement manned by two G.I.'s.

>   DAVIS
>   Okay, sir. That's it. Let's go.

They start away - going left to right.

193   WIDE SHOT

The patrol numbering ten men leaves the front line position; they walk in single file, led by Sgt. Davis and Parker - left to right.

194   CLOSE SHOT

The men pass by CAMERA - left to right. Sgt. Davis is in the lead followed by Parker. Among the others we recognize Sam, Romeo, Pinto and a couple of G.I.'s seen in the earlier scene in the regimental aid station.

                                        (CONTINUED)

64.

194	CONTINUED:

	The rear is brought up by a medic, whom we also saw in the earlier scene. The men are holding their weapons at port arms...

195	LONG SHOT

	The patrol is disappearing into the dark forest - going left to right...

EXT. WOODED SLOPE OF MONTE ADONE   NIGHT

196	MED. SHOT

	Through the night-dark forest the men of the patrol quietly, walk along - going left to right.

197	CLOSE SHOT SGT. DAVIS

	He looks around alertly as he leads the patrol on.

198	CLOSE SHOT PARKER

	He too looks watchful.

199	CLOSE TWO SHOT ROMEO, SAM

	Cautiously they walk along - left to right.

200	MED. WIDE SHOT PATROL

	They are nearing the small depression of a dry stream bed... Walking left to right in single file they begin to cross.

201	CLOSE SHOT G.I. COMBAT BOOTS

	Carefully they negotiate the stones and rocks of the dry stream bed - going left to right...

					MATCH CUT TO:

EXT. ROCKY AREA OF THE SLOPE OF MONTE ADONE   NIGHT

202	CLOSE SHOT GERMAN HOBNAILED BOOTS

	Going right to left the boots - three pairs of them - skirt a rugged boulder.

203 WIDER ANGLE

We see Heinrich, Richter and Krim making their way across the rough terrain - moving right to left.

204 CLOSE SHOT

The men pass by CAMERA in CLOSEUPS - going right to left. First Heinrich, then Richter and Krim.

205 ANOTHER ANGLE

The three men are working their way onwards. Heinrich stops; he motions for the men to take cover; they do.

206 CLOSE SHOT   HEINRICH

He looks through his binoculars - facing left.

207 CLOSE SHOT   RICHTER

Facing left he is grasping his Schmeisser machine pistol firmly.

208 CLOSEUP   RICHTER'S HANDS

They are tense on the gun.

MATCH CUT TO:

EXT. MONTE ADONE WOODS   NIGHT

209 CLOSEUP HANDS

They are tense on a Thompson sub-machine gun...CAMERA DOLLIES OUT to see Romeo - facing right - crouched behind a tree, watching.

210 MED. SHOT   SGT. DAVIS

He, too, is crouching - facing right; he motions silently for the men to move forward.

211 WIDE SHOT

The men move out - left to right.

66.

212   CLOSE SHOT   PARKER (DAVIS)

Close by Davis, Parker is moving on carefully, making his way up the rocky slope of Monte Adone - going left to right.

213   ANOTHER ANGLE   MED. WIDE SHOT

The patrol is moving slowly left to right...Sgt. Davis holds up his hand - and the men stop - taking cover...Parker joins Davis.

214   TWO SHOT   PARKER, DAVIS

Without a word Davis points ahead.

215   SHOT ACROSS PARKER AND DAVIS (R.P.)

In the b.g. can be seen the dead ruins of Santa Angelo.

216   TWO SHOT   PARKER, DAVIS

Parker raises his field glasses and observes the quiet, deserted village.

217   SPECIAL EFFECTS SHOT   POV PARKER THROUGH FIELD GLASSES
       PAN

There is no movement to be seen in the ruined, empty village.

218   CLOSEUP PARKER

He is watching through his U.S. Army Field glasses - looking left to right.

MATCH CUT TO:

EXT. SLOPE OF MONTE ADONE   NIGHT

219   CLOSEUP   HEINRICH

He is looking towards Santa Angelo through his German Field glasses - right to left. CAMERA PULLS OUT to a THREE SHOT revealing Richter and Krim. Heinrich lowers his glasses; he indicates a piece of high ground to the west of the village.

                HEINRICH
              (to Richter)
    The high ground is over there. To
    the west of Santa Angelo.

(CONTINUED)

219   CONTINUED:

> RICHTER
> Right.
>
> HEINRICH
> Let's move out.

The three men move on. CAMERA HOLDS in a MED. WIDE SHOT until the men are all OUT OF FRAME.

MATCH CUT TO:

EXT. MONTE ADONE WOODS (SAME LOCATION AS LAST SCENE WITH PATROL) NIGHT

220   MED. WIDE SHOT

At first it seems the area is deserted; then a small movement catches the eye.

221   CLOSER ANGLE   TWO SHOT   PARKER, DAVIS

They are lying in concealment - watching the little village ahead - looking left to right.

> DAVIS
> That's Santa Angelo, sir. Dead as a door nail - and about as much left of it!
>
> PARKER
> Looks deserted.
>
> DAVIS
> Let's go have a look-see.

He raises himself up - and motions for the rest of the patrol to move out, in the direction of Santa Angelo.

222   MED. WIDE SHOT

The patrol is moving forward - left to right - towards the ruins of Santa Angelo - towards the booby-trap infested ambush, which already has claimed the lives of the men of Sgt. Ryan's ill-fated patrol!

EXT. RUINS OF SANTA ANGELO VILLAGE (SAME AS OPENING SCENE)   NIGHT

223   CLOSE SHOT   PAN

We again see the small, wooden roadside shrine so common in many European countries, with the V-shaped roof and the carved figure of the Madonna.

(CONTINUED)

68.

223 CONTINUED:

Her arms are gently, lovingly cradled in front of her, and she is serenely gazing down at the child belonging there. But her arms are empty. The Christ Child has been blasted away by a shell fragment, along with half of one of the Madonna's arms and part of the shrine itself. CAMERA SLOWLY PANS OFF the war-mutilated shrine, across the ruins of a stone shack to a pile of rubble and debris.

224 ANOTHER ANGLE

The patrol is crawling towards the village; they stop and take cover among the rubble.

225 CLOSER ANGLE

Parker crawls to join Davis.

226 TWO SHOT   PARKER, DAVIS

> PARKER
> Sergeant. A suggestion. I know I'm just along for the ride - but how about scouting that high ground over there to the west of the village? Looks like it might be the place, where the partisan girl saw that communications wire.

Sgt. Davis looks towards the indicated high ground - then back at the village; he seems undecided - finally...

> DAVIS
> Okay, sir.

He makes a "change direction of advance" sign to his men.

227 WIDER ANGLE

The men of the patrol back away from the ruins - and start to move off in the direction of the wooded high ground to the west.

EXT. WOODED HIGH GROUND OF MONTE ADONE   NIGHT

228 MED. SHOT

Crouched low the men of the patrol slowly, quietly move through the sparsely wooded area.

229 ANOTHER ANGLE

　　　The men are moving on.

230 CLOSE SHOT   PARKER

　　　Alertly he moves through the underbrush.

231 CLOSE SHOT   DAVIS

　　　He looks about cautiously, as he walks on.

232 CLOSE SHOT   ROMEO

　　　He stops to listen; he looks around; then he starts to move on...suddenly he stops - quickly he turns to look at something on the ground he almost missed...He bends down to examine it.

233 CLOSEUP   WIRE ON GROUND

　　　It is almost hidden by leaves and shrubs. Romeo's hand carefully pulls it free.

234 CLOSE SHOT   ROMEO

　　　He straightens up.

> ROMEO
> (in a hoarse whisper)
> Sergeant! Over here!

235 MED. SHOT   DAVIS, PARKER

> ROMEO (o.s.)
> (whisper)
> Over here!

　　　The two men at once make for the sound of Romeo's call.

236 MED. SHOT

　　　Parker and Davis join Romeo; he shows them the wire; they examine it; it is running off in both directions.

> PARKER
> That's it!
>
> DAVIS
> (to Romeo)
> Get Pinto over here. On the double!

(CONTINUED)

70.

236   CONTINUED:

Romeo turns and calls in a low voice.

>   ROMEO
> Sam! Get Pinto. Shake it up!

237   CLOSE SHOT   SAM

He is crouched in concealment behind a bush; he turns and calls softly:

>   SAM
> Pinto! Over there! Get the lead out!

238   CLOSE SHOT   PINTO   PAN SHOT

He hurries through the forest to Parker, Davis and Romeo at the communications wire.

239   FOUR SHOT

Quickly Pinto brings out a listening device; hurriedly, expertly he attaches it to the wire - and hands Parker the earphones; Parker begins to listen;

240   CLOSEUP   PARKER

He is listening intently.

241   CLOSEUP   PINTO

He is watching Parker suspensefully.

242   CLOSEUP   DAVIS

He, too, is watching.

243   FOUR SHOT

With a look of disappointment Parker shakes his head. The men look let down. Suddenly there is a small noise in the trees - from a direction and a distance, where no patrol members can be. Sgt. Davis and Parker glance alertly towards the sound, then Davis motions a "take cover" sign, and instantly, noiselessly, the men literally melt into the shrubs and trees, as they take cover...

244   CLOSE TWO SHOT   PARKER, DAVIS

Intently they peer through their concealment in the direction of the sound...All is quiet.

245   LONG SHOT POV   PARKER, DAVIS

The forest is dark and silent; nothing moves for a while - then - all at once an indistinctive shadow can be seen moving briefly, before the woods are quiet again.

246   TWO SHOT   PARKER, DAVIS

Quickly they look at one another; they get their weapons ready.

247   WIDE ANGLE   FOREST

We know the patrol is lying in concealment - but we can see nothing...Then - through the night dark forest three figures can be seen slowly approaching; crouched and moving with great caution - one by one they come into the clearing area of the woods; carefully, quietly they press on.

248   TWO SHOT   PARKER, DAVIS

All at once Davis gives a mighty cry - and with Parker he leaps to his feet from concealment.

            DAVIS
    Go!

249   WIDE ANGLE

All around the three figures in the center the men of the patrol jump up from their cover. The three intruders are surrounded - but they do not give up. A voice barks:

            VOICE
    Deckung nehmen!

250   THE FIGHT

The fight will be routined with coverage and intercuts as needed. The three Germans throw themselves to the ground; a brief gun battle ensues - during which Sgt. Davis is hit by a bullet in his shoulder. The G.I.'s charge - and hand to hand combat results; at one point one of the Germans is just about to shoot Sam, when a gun blow by Parker knocks him cold...And it is over.

(CONTINUED)

71.

250 CONTINUED:

Sgt. Davis and one other man have been wounded; two of the Germans have been killed and the third - knocked out by Parker - lies unconscious on the ground.

251 MED. CLOSE SHOT   PARKER, GERMAN

Parker bends over the unconscious German - hiding his face from CAMERA.

              PARKER
  Medic!

252 WIDER ANGLE

The medic quickly comes over from having attended Davis; he bends over the German.

253 CLOSE SHOT   MEDIC, PARKER

The medic is examining the unconscious man; he looks up at Parker.

              MEDIC
  Just a beaut of a bump, sir. He'll be okay.

He straightens up to reveal the German's face; CAMERA ZOOMS IN to a CLOSEUP...It is Lt. Otto Heinrich!

254 CLOSEUP   PARKER

He is looking with great interest at the German officer.

255 CLOSEUP   HEINRICH

He is unconscious. CAMERA MOVES IN AND PANS to a CLOSE SHOT of the shoulder strap on his uniform; it shows the characteristic, horse-show-shaped braid of a German officer's shoulder strap....the color is red...red for artillery!

              MATCH CUT TO:

INT. IPW ROOM IN SANTA MARIA SCHOOL HOUSE   NIGHT

256 CLOSEUP COLONEL'S EAGLE INSIGNIA ON UNIFORM SHOULDER

CAMERA PULLS BACK QUICKLY to a TWO SHOT of Colonel Bradford and Parker standing before the blackboard map; during:

              (CONTINUED)

256   CONTINUED:

>   PARKER
>   ...His shoulder-strap shows him to
>   be an officer - a Lieutenant. His
>   I.D. disc says Lt. Otto Heinrich.
>   The color of his braid is red...
>
>   BRADFORD
>   Artillery! What would an artillery
>   officer be doing up front?
>
>   PARKER
>   Nothing. Unless he was an artillery
>   observer...
>
>   BRADFORD
>   Couldn't be better!

He turns and walks to Parker's desk.

257   WIDER ANGLE

Bradford comes up to Parker's desk; Parker follows. At the desk is Hicks, readying some papers. Bradford picks up the capture report and glances through it. He looks up at Parker.

>   BRADFORD
>   (with a grin)
>   Knocked him out yourself, eh?

Parker grins back.

>   PARKER
>   (grinning)
>   I wish I could say I knew exactly
>   what I was doing!
>
>   BRADFORD
>   Main thing is - we got him. That's
>   what counts.
>
>   PARKER
>   (soberly)
>   Provided he comes up with the
>   information. He may not be inclined
>   to accommodate.
>
>   BRADFORD
>   Go to work on him. Looks like you
>   won't get much rest tonight.
>
>   PARKER
>   Hicks'll keep me supplied with
>   black coffee.

(CONTINUED)

257   CONTINUED:

> HICKS
> Would the Colonel care for some coffee too?

> BRADFORD
> Volunteering for K.P.?

> HICKS
> Haven't volunteered for <u>anything</u> since basic training!

Outside the open door can be heard the approaching footsteps of several men.

> PARKER
> They're bringing him in, sir.

> BRADFORD
> (seriously)
> Get us that Kraut battery, Dirk!

He leaves...CAMERA HOLDS AND TIGHTENS to a TWO SHOT of Parker and Hicks. Parker quickly looks over his desk; then he meets Hicks' eyes...Already the distant rumble of motorized equipment can be heard from outside, as the first elements of Corps Forward are pulling into the village. The men react to the noise.

> HICKS
> Corps is starting to come in...

> PARKER
> (he nods; quietly)
> Okay, Jim. Bring him in...

Hicks leaves.

<u>INT. CORRIDOR OUTSIDE IPW ROOM   NIGHT</u>

258   MED. SHOT

Romeo and Sam, both still in patrol combat gear and dirty from the skirmish, are guarding Heinrich. The German looks only the slightest bit apprehensive - but holds himself erect in a very military manner. We feel an inherent self-confidence bordering on arrogance in his extremely correct bearing...Hicks comes from the IPW room; he beckons to the G.I.'s.

> HICKS
> Okay. Bring him in.

Sam and Romeo motion for Heinrich to go in.

(CONTINUED)

258   CONTINUED:

>   ROMEO
>   Move it, buddy, move it!

They start towards the door.

INT. IPW ROOM IN SANTA MARIA SCHOOL HOUSE   NIGHT

259   MED. CLOSE SHOT   PARKER

He is seated behind his desk; he looks stern and grim...He is looking towards the door; there is the SOUND of footsteps. Parker reacts.

260   ANGLE FEATURING DOOR

Hicks enters, followed by Heinrich and the two G.I.'s. Hicks stops inside the door; he snaps to attention and renders Parker a snappy salute.

>   HICKS
>   Sir! The prisoner!

Parker returns the salute.

>   PARKER
>   Very good, Sergeant.

Hicks turns to the G.I.'s.

>   HICKS
>   Okay, you guys. We'll take it
>   from here.

Sam and Romeo leave the room reluctantly; Hicks closes the door behind them and remains standing next to it - as Heinrich stiffly steps towards Parker.

261   CLOSER ANGLE   HEINRICH, PARKER

Heinrich clicks his heels; salutes Parker and announces:

>   HEINRICH
>   <u>Leutnant Otto Heinrich</u>!

Parker returns the salute informally; he has adopted a relaxed, easy attitude.

>   PARKER
>   <u>Guten Abend, Herr Leutnant. Ich bin
>   Hauptman Parker.</u>

(CONTINUED)

261   CONTINUED:

                    HEINRICH
          I understand English, sir.

                    PARKER
          That so? Fine. Please sit down.

Heinrich is a little bewildered by Parker's casual, informal
attitude; somewhat hesitantly he sits down in a chair across
from Parker. The IPW takes a cigarette from a pack and
lights it; he offers one to Heinrich.

                    PARKER
          Smoke?

                    HEINRICH
               (after a brief
                hesitation)
          If I may take the liberty.

Heinrich extracts a cigarette from the pack a little
clumsily; he looks for a match; Parker offers him his
lighter.

                    PARKER
          Here.

                    HEINRICH
          Thank you, sir.

Heinrich lights the cigarette; he takes a deep puff - and
it is obvious, he enjoys the real tobacco very much. Parker
observes him keenly.

                    PARKER
          Looks like the war is over for you.

                    HEINRICH
               (stiffly)
          Unfortunately, Captain. I'd rather
          be with my unit.

                    PARKER
          Your battery, you mean.

Heinrich glances quickly at Parker.

                    PARKER
               (smiling)
          It's alright, Lieutenant. I know
          you're an artillery man.
               (he indicates the
                shoulder straps)
          Red - stands for artillery in any
          army I know of.

                                        (CONTINUED)

261 CONTINUED: - 2

Heinrich makes no reply.

> PARKER
> (conversationally)
> Must be an unpleasant experience -
> being taken prisoner.

Heinrich says nothing.

> PARKER
> But then - I suppose you were lucky.
> I understand your men were killed...

The subtle inference that Heinrich could have prevented this puts the man on the defensive.

> HEINRICH
> We were ambushed. Very much
> outnumbered.

> PARKER
> Then there were only the three of
> you?

> HEINRICH
> (touch of arrogance)
> Sorry, Captain!

Parker does not make an issue of it; he smiles.

> PARKER
> Just wondering...

> HEINRICH
> Sir. We might as well understand
> one another. I am a Prisoner of War.
> I shall give you no information other
> than my name, rank and serial number.

> PARKER
> (pleasantly)
> How about some coffee? You will
> join me?

Heinrich is puzzled by Parker's easy-going attitude.

> HEINRICH
> (formally)
> If I may. Thank you.

> PARKER
> Sergeant Hicks!

Hicks steps into the picture; he acts in a strict military manner.

(CONTINUED)

261 CONTINUED: - 3

HICKS
Sir?

PARKER
Get us some coffee...And - is there something to eat?

HICKS
I'll bring something, sir.

He leaves. Heinrich is beginning to relax.

HEINRICH
On my way here I had a chance to observe quite a lot of your equipment ...You seem to be well supplied.

PARKER
We are. One of our secret weapons - production capacity!

Heinrich looks up sharply at the mention of "secret weapon."

HEINRICH
It is a great pity you Americans had to get into the war. We are not enemies. We had no conflict.

PARKER
(easily)
We just didn't want to wait for _our_ turn.

HEINRICH
Your turn?
(he suddenly realizes Parker's meaning)
But the Fuehrer said...

PARKER
(pleasantly interrupting)
The Fuehrer also said he wouldn't go into Austria, and Czechoslovakia, and Poland...Need I go on?

Hicks arrives with two cups of coffee, some Army baked bread, butter and cheese.

PARKER
Ah - here we are.

Heinrich drinks his coffee; it is an obvious pleasure for him.

(CONTINUED)

261   CONTINUED: - 4

>   HEINRICH
> Real coffee...

Parker offers him some bread; Heinrich accepts; he looks at it.

>   HEINRICH
> Cake?

>   PARKER
> Just American bread.

Heinrich looks impressed despite himself. He is getting thoroughly caught up in the carefully planned conversational - almost casual - aspect of the interrogation.

>   HEINRICH
> It is very good, sir.

>   PARKER
>   (conversationally)
> Where is your home town in Germany?

>   HEINRICH
> May I respectfully point out that according to the Geneva Conventions...

Suddenly Parker's entire attitude changes; his voice becomes sharp as a knife; his manner commanding, authoritative - almost threatening..!

>   PARKER
> Geneva Conventions! Did you observe them last December during the Ardennes Offensive? When hundreds of our men were shot with their hands tied behind their backs - mowed down by your SS?!

Heinrich is completely taken aback.

>   HEINRICH
> That's propaganda!

>   PARKER
>   (ominously)
> Are you contradicting the official findings of our Supreme Headquarters?

Parker's complete change of attitude has a profound effect on Heinrich. He loses some of his self-confidence; tries to cover it with military formality.

(CONTINUED)

261 CONTINUED: - 5

> HEINRICH
> If it pleases the Captain, I do not wish to appear disrespectful, but...

> PARKER
> (interrupting; sharply)
> Lieutenant! You are a Prisoner of War - subject to our orders. Right now my orders! Is that understood?

> HEINRICH
> (tight-lipped)
> Yes, sir.

> PARKER
> You've lost the war! Any more casualties - American and German - is a criminal waste.

> HEINRICH
> The war is not won yet - by either side. The Fuehrer has told us he has a secret weapon...

> PARKER
> Nonsense! Don't you think, if your Fuehrer had a secret weapon he'd use it? Now?!...

Heinrich reacts to this statement - almost exactly what he himself said to Major Schiller.

> PARKER
> Anyway, it is of the utmost importance to both you and us that hostilities be terminated as soon as possible. We are under orders to use all possible means to achieve this end - and your cooperation will be expected. There is certain information, I want to check, before I let you go. What is your unit?

> HEINRICH
> (shocked)
> I cannot tell you that!

> PARKER
> You are under orders to do so!

> HEINRICH
> I can give you no information.

> PARKER
> Perhaps you don't understand me. I'm giving you a direct order!

(CONTINUED)

261   CONTINUED: - 6

                    HEINRICH
          I cannot recognize such an order,
          sir.

                    PARKER
                (coldly)
          You realize, of course, that this
          makes you guilty of insubordination.

Heinrich does not answer.

                    PARKER
          Answer me, Lieutenant! What is your
          unit? Where is your battery located?

                    HEINRICH
          I have nothing to say, sir.

                    PARKER
          If you persist in being uncooperative,
          you'll have to bear the consequences..
          Hicks!

Hicks snaps to.

                    HICKS
          Sir?

                    PARKER
          The tag!

Hicks at once removes the PW tag from Heinrich, making him
stand up; he gives it to Parker. Once again the large "R"
is imprinted on a PW tag...Heinrich stands erect...and
silent, although he obviously sees the "R"...

                    PARKER
          You know what that "R" means,
          Lieutenant? It means that when
          we're through with you - you'll
          be sent to the Russians...unless
          you decide to become cooperative.

Heinrich grows pale; he clenches his teeth; then he snaps
to attention.

                    HEINRICH
          May I respectfully repeat my
          request for evacuation to the rear.

                    PARKER
          You'll go back, when I'm good and
          ready to send you back...Or when
          you tell me the location of your
          battery!

                                        (CONTINUED)

261   CONTINUED: - 7

>   HEINRICH
>   (firmly)
>   I cannot do that.
>
>   PARKER
>   (to Hicks)
>   Take him away.

Hicks starts to lead Heinrich away.

>   PARKER
>   Don't put him with the others in the
>   PW cage. Put him in the storeroom
>   right here - under guard. It's still
>   the safest building in Santa Maria.

Heinrich stiffens at the mention of the name of the village. He turns to Parker.

>   HEINRICH
>   Excuse me, Captain. I did not know
>   where I am. It was dark. This is
>   Santa Maria?
>
>   PARKER
>   (curtly)
>   Yes.

Heinrich reacts.

262   CLOSE SHOT   HEINRICH

He looks around the room; his eyes widen with grim realization.

263   SHOT POV HEINRICH

In a corner of the room are all the piled up school desks!

264   CLOSEUP   HEINRICH

He looks stricken!

INT. S-2 ROOM IN SANTA MARIA SCHOOL HOUSE   NIGHT

265   MED. SHOT   FEATURING DOOR

It suddenly bursts open, and Colonel Bradford storms in; he has obviously just been roused from sleep; he looks grumpy. CAMERA CARRIES him to Parker and Armstrong, who are waiting for him.

(CONTINUED)

265   CONTINUED:

>   BRADFORD
> Well!? You got me up in the middle
> of my two hour rest. It'd better
> be good!

>   ARMSTRONG
>   (he seems smugly
>   pleased)
> I'm afraid it isn't, Colonel.
> Parker here hasn't been able to get
> a thing!

>   BRADFORD
>   (sharply; to Parker)
> Why not?

>   PARKER
> I didn't really expect too much
> first time around, sir. He's an
> intelligent man, every inch an
> officer, well indoctrinated -
> Hitler Youth, that sort of thing...

>   BRADFORD
> Did you get anything out of him at
> all? I want it on the line!

>   PARKER
> He is a forward artillery observer
> alright. Air Corps, judging from
> his uniform. And it's the Air Corps
> that has the 88's. They used them
> primarily for anti-aircraft, but
> now they're also being used for
> tactical support. He might well be
> from the battery we're after.

>   BRADFORD
> Then find out where it is, damn it!

>   PARKER
> I'll do my best...

>   ARMSTRONG
> That may not be good enough, Parker!

>   PARKER
> May _I_ be the judge of that, Major?

>   ARMSTRONG
> Your lily-livered methods won't get
> you anywhere. There's only one way
> to fight those bastards, Captain.
> Be as cussed - as unscrupulous - as
> they are!

(CONTINUED)

265   CONTINUED: - 2

> PARKER
> And what does that do, Major? Make them right? Or us wrong?!

> ARMSTRONG
> (angrily)
> What's the matter with you? Can't you sacrifice just one little principle?

> PARKER
> Just one? And then another? And one more? Where do we stop?

> ARMSTRONG
> I'm sure all you have to do is show him we can be rough too...

> PARKER
> And if that's not enough...?

> ARMSTRONG
> Damn it, man! What's more important? The creature comfort of one Kraut - or a couple of hundred of our boys ending up wearing mattress covers!

> BRADFORD
> That's enough!
> (to Parker)
> You're the IPW. You get the information!

> PARKER
> Yes, sir...I have a hunch...

Armstrong snorts contemptuously.

> PARKER
> (continues)
> There's something about Lieutenant Heinrich...I had the definite feeling, he...he seemed worried at the end...

> ARMSTRONG
> Worried! Don't scare him too badly, Parker!

> BRADFORD
> (sharply)
> Alright, Major!
> (to Parker)
> Work on him. And get me results!

(CONTINUED)

265 CONTINUED: - 3

                    PARKER
          Yes, sir.

                    BRADFORD
          That's all.

                    PARKER
          Yes, sir.

Parker leaves the room.

EXT. SANTA MARIA SCHOOL HOUSE   NIGHT

266 MED. SHOT

Parker comes out of the building; he stops.

267 MED. CLOSEUP PARKER

For a moment he stands in deep thought; then he seems to take a grip on himself - and he starts off, walking out of picture...

EXT. AID STATION   NIGHT

268 WIDE SHOT

Parker comes down the street; he enters the Aid Station.

INT. AID STATION COLLECTION ROOM   NIGHT

269 MED. SHOT FEATURING DOOR

Parker appears in the door; he looks around - sees what he is looking for and walks towards it. CAMERA CARRIES HIM through the ward, past a few men on cots to Sgt. Davis; he, too, is lying on a cot - his shoulder bandaged; he grins, as he sees Parker.

CAMERA HOLDS in a TWO SHOT.

                    PARKER
          How's the shoulder?

                    DAVIS
          Never touched me! I'm just dead-
          beating here!

                    PARKER
                (with a grin)
          Always figured you for a real
          goldbrick!

(CONTINUED)

269   CONTINUED:

>   DAVIS
> That guy, we brought back. He be
> any good to you?

A fleeting frown clouds Parker's face; he tries to be cheerful - with only partial success.

>   PARKER
> Sure will. Just what the Old Man
> ordered.

>   DAVIS
> Get him to spill his guts, Captain!
> We'd sure appreciate that...me - and
> Smitty over there.

He nods towards another cot.

270   SHOT   COT   POV DAVIS

The cot is partly hidden by a make-shift screen.

271   TWO SHOT   PARKER, DAVIS

>   PARKER
> How's he doing?

>   DAVIS
>   (soberly)
> Tell you the truth, sir. I don't
> think he'll make it.

Parker looks grim.

>   PARKER
> You take it easy.

>   DAVIS
> Sure thing. And - Sir...I know
> you'll get that Kraut to talk!

Parker nods soberly; then he leaves. CAMERA HOLDS on Davis; as he looks after the officer.

EXT. AID STATION   NIGHT

272   MED. SHOT

Parker comes out; he looks thoughtfully grave; he walks off.

87.

EXT. SANTA MARIA STREET   NIGHT

273   MED. SHOT

Parker comes walking down the street...There is the quick, sudden "whoosh" of an incoming 88 artillery shell - and the crashing EXPLOSION, as it hits nearby...The nightly shelling is beginning - as dependable as Hicks' grandfather clock.

274   ANOTHER ANGLE

Parker looks around briefly...Other soldiers and civilians are hurriedly taking cover...Quickly Parker runs into a bombed-out house for cover.

INT. HOUSE   NIGHT

275   MED. SHOT

The house is empty, deserted; Parker comes running in from the street; there are some stairs leading down to the cellar - and he hurries down, just as another shell lands outside.

INT. CELLAR OF EMPTY HOUSE   NIGHT

276   SHOT

It is not a large place; there are a few crates and barrels; a pile of sacks in one corner, a small window set high in the heavy wall.

277   MED. WIDE SHOT

The place is dark; Parker comes down the stairs; he stands for a moment to get used to the darkness - then he notices a candle stump on an overturned barrel; he walks to it.

278   CLOSE SHOT   PARKER

He lights the candle with his lighter - and holds it up. He suddenly reacts with surprise.

279   SHOT   POV PARKER

There - imprisoned in the flickering light from the candle flame stands - Rina...She, too, has sought refuge in the cellar from the shells.

(CONTINUED)

279   CONTINUED:

> PARKER
> Rina! What are you doing here?
>
> RINA
> Same as you, Capitane, get away from the shells.
>
> PARKER
> (looking around)
> Are we alone?
>
> RINA
> (suspiciously)
> Yes...Why do you ask...
>
> PARKER
> Just wondering.
> (looking at the girl)
> You know, Rina...you are a very beautiful girl in spite of that outfit...

Parker looks admiringly at the girl, who misunderstands his admiration and backs away from the man.

> PARKER
> (continuing)
> There must be a real woman under that partisan get-up...
>
> RINA
> (still retreating)
> Soldiers! All alike - Germans, Italians, Americans...
>
> PARKER
> (beginning to under-
> stand the girl's
> thoughts)
> But Rina...

280   TWO SHOT

Just then another shell lands, close enough to rattle the entire house - sending dust and plaster raining from the ceiling...Parker quickly looks around; he notices a stone archway; without a word he grabs the girl and pulls her with him, as he takes cover under the comparative safety of the massive arch - just as another shell sends loosened masonry crashing down from the ceiling.

281   CLOSE TWO SHOT

When the plaster dust clears away, the two people, standing close together, regard each other...Parker with frank admiration; Rina with eyes burning with sullen suspicion and contempt. Parker glances around the cellar.

>   PARKER
> You okay?
>
>   RINA
> Yes.
>
>   PARKER
> Good...Come on...

There is a world of bitter deadness and disillusionment in her lovely face and voice. Parker makes a move toward her. Suddenly she flares at him.

>   RINA
> Alright, soldier! I know what you want! I do not care! I help you!

Vehemently she rips open her blouse and stands defiantly before him.

282   CLOSEUP   RINA

Her face is a study in torment, anger, revulsion - and defiance.

283   CLOSEUP   PARKER

He looks solemnly at the girl.

284   TWO SHOT

Slowly Parker reaches for the girl; gently he closes her ripped blouse - and with a little shiver she hugs her arms around her. Earnestly, compassionately and without a word Parker looks at her...a lovely, wretched little figure huddled against the cold, hard stone. And suddenly the defiance, the bitterness, the hardness falls away from the girl's face like an unwanted mask - and with a little sob she finds refuge in Parker's arms. The tears come freely and silently. Another shell lands a little further away - unnoticed by the two young people, as Parker gently lets Rina sit down.

>   PARKER
>   (softly)
> Rina...Easy now...easy...

(CONTINUED)

284 CONTINUED:

Rina suddenly draws away from him; she looks at him with huge, burning eyes.

                  RINA
Easy! Nothing is easy - except killing Nazis!

Parker regards the girl with concern.

                  PARKER
That's not for you...It's - it's much too dangerous...

                  RINA
           (with a shrug)
So one day they kill me...No matter.

                  PARKER
Tell me, Rina, how did you get into this? Where are your folks?

                  RINA
           (harshly)
I am alone! What I do is my business.

                  PARKER
And your parents? Don't you think they worry about you?

                  RINA
           (bitterly; cynically)
My parents?! You want to know..! Alright - I tell you.

285 CLOSE TWO SHOT (INTERCUTS AS DESIRED)

                  RINA
From I was seven years old my "father" was the Fascist State - my "mother" the political orphanage!

                  PARKER
I'm sorry, Rina...I'm sorry you lost your parents so young...

                  RINA
Lost them?! You want to know how? One night they came and took them away...I never saw them again...

                  PARKER
Who - took them away?

                             (CONTINUED)

285	CONTINUED:

                RINA
            (her voice filled
             with hate)
    The "Ovra!"...The Secret Police!
           (in a low voice)
    They were denounced. For - thoughts
    against the State...

                PARKER
            (sincerely)
    I think I understand, Rina..

He looks at her with deep compassion.

                PARKER
    But you mustn't let it ruin you...
    your life...Think of your parents -
    not of the miserable wretch, who
    denounced them.

                RINA
    It is not possible.

With dark agony in her huge eyes Rina looks at Parker.

                RINA
            (torture in her voice)
    You know who did it?....I did!

Stunned, Parker looks at the girl.

                RINA
    <u>I</u> did it! <u>I</u> denounced my parents!
    My teacher had taught me. I did
    not know then, <u>what</u> I was doing...

She looks straight at Parker; her eyes flashing.

                RINA
    But - now I know...And I hate it!

She huddles away from Parker in self-loathing; gently he takes her hands.

                PARKER
    Don't blame yourself, Rina...You
    just said you didn't know what you
    were doing.

                RINA
    It was my fault...I killed them!

                          (CONTINUED)

285   CONTINUED: - 2

> PARKER
> (gently)
> Rina, be fair with yourself. I'm sure the only one who puts any blame on you is you yourself!

Rina looks up at him.

> RINA
> (in a small voice)
> You - don't...?

> PARKER
> I don't.

For a long moment Rina looks at Parker. Then she gives a deep, unconscious sigh - and the tenseness seems to go from her. Parker draws her closer to him...Outside the shelling is long past, but the two young people have no thoughts of leaving the sanctuary of the dark cellar.

> PARKER
> Rina, promise me one thing. Promise me you'll leave Volpe's band. No more partisan stuff...

> RINA
> (seriously)
> I cannot do that. I do have a debt to pay. A duty...
> (she looks searchingly at him)
> Like you. You have a duty, too...

> PARKER
> (nods thoughtfully)
> Yes...I only wish I knew the _right_ way to carry it out...

> RINA
> You are thinking of your prisoner.

Parker nods.

> RINA
> Volpe says you are soft. That you won't - _make_ him talk...be rough... He says _that_ is what you _must_ do.

> PARKER
> What do you think?

(CONTINUED)

285   CONTINUED: - 3

>   RINA
>   (slowly)
>   The Secret Police - they tortured
>   their prisoners. They were not -
>   soft...And I hated them!
>
>   PARKER
>   I wish I knew that I was right...and
>   not Volpe...or Major Armstrong.
>
>   RINA
>   Perhaps - perhaps you cannot make a
>   rule that must always be right...
>   Perhaps each case must be given a
>   decision all its own...If that is
>   so - what about this prisoner?
>
>   PARKER
>   (he looks disturbed)
>   How the devil do I know?! Right
>   now - I hate the Krauts. If I
>   decide to get rough with that guy,
>   that hate is bound to have
>   influenced me...but it sure as hell
>   doesn't make it right!

Rina looks at the IPW officer with genuine concern; for the moment she has completely forgotten her preoccupation with herself; the harshness and bitterness have left her - and she has emerged a warm and vibrant woman...

>   PARKER
>   (miserably)
>   Damn Armstrong anyway! Why did he
>   have to open that can of beans?!

Rina is completely conscious of Parker's mental struggle with himself; she deliberately tries to lighten the atmosphere a little.

>   RINA
>   Don't be angry with the Major...
>   I do remember some of the things
>   my father used to say...He said:
>   You should always be tolerant with
>   a person, who disagrees with you.
>   After all - he has a right to his
>   own ridiculous opinion!

Despite himself Parker grins...and the girl responds with a radiant smile. Their eyes meet - and slowly the smiles fade away - as the two young people are drawn to each other, in an ardent embrace.

(CONTINUED)

285 CONTINUE:D - 4

They kiss longingly - all their pent-up passion and emotion released...They stay in a close embrace.

                    PARKER
                   (softly)
          Rina...

                    RINA
                (in a whisper)
          Carino mio...

Again they kiss - hungrily, almost fiercely...He kisses her lips, her throat - and bends down - down...And CAMERA DOLLIES IN to a CLOSEUP of Rina, as she slowly turns and bends her head back, eyes closed, lips parted...

CAMERA PANS the darkened, silent cellar - and PANS UP to a CLOSE SHOT of a small, square window set at ground level in the thick stone wall; all the glass panes and a couple of the wooden struts are broken; outside it is pitch dark... Gradually it gets lighter.

                                        MATCH CUT TO:

INT. SCHOOL HOUSE STORE ROOM   DAWN

286 CLOSE SHOT   SMALL, HALF-MOON SHAPED WINDOW

Placed high in the heavy wall it has a couple of sturdy, iron bars set in it; no glass. Outside can be seen the grey light of dawn. CAMERA PULLS OUT to a MED. SHOT revealing Heinrich; he is dozing on a pile of sacks. We see the heavy, wooden door to the cell.

Suddenly - with the shock of an explosion - the door is flung open; startled, Heinrich jerks awake; crouching against the wall he stares at the door.

287 MED. SHOT   DOOR   POV HEINRICH

In the doorway stands Parker; he looks dark and scowling; behind him stand Sam and Romeo; grim-faced they hold their rifles on the ready. Parker snaps.

                    PARKER
          On your feet!

288 MED. SHOT

Heinrich scrambles to his feet; Parker nods to the two men with him; they enter the cell.

                                        (CONTINUED)

288 CONTINUED:

                    PARKER
          Put your hands behind your neck!

Heinrich, bewildered, a little apprehensive, does not move fast enough for Parker.

                    PARKER
                    (like a shot)
          Move!

With an ugly look Sam points his gun squarely at Heinrich; the German obeys the command.

                    PARKER
          Let's go.

Abruptly he turns on his heel; Romeo prods Heinrich, who goes after Parker - closely followed by the two G.I.'s. As Sam leaves he slams the door behind him.

EXT. SANTA MARIA SCHOOL HOUSE   DAWN

289 MED. WIDE SHOT

Parker, Heinrich and the two G.I.'s leave the School House and walk towards the village square. There is general activity in the streets and in the square.

EXT. SANTA MARIA VILLAGE SQUARE   DAWN

290 MED. SHOT

Parker and his men are marching Heinrich through the square. Suddenly a deep voice calls o.s.

                    VOICE
          Captain!

Parker stops and looks.

291 LONG SHOT   POV PARKER

Across the square stands the group of partisans; Volpe, Tony, Rina and the others; they look grim and foreboding. Volpe again calls to Parker.

                    VOLPE
          Captain Parker!

292   GROUP SHOT   PARKER, HEINRICH, ROMEO, SAM   PAN

Parker turns to the men.

> PARKER
> Keep him here.

He walks away towards the partisans; CAMERA PANS him, as he makes his way across the square through the general activity; he joins the partisans in a LONG SHOT. Volpe and Parker begin an animated conversation; they look across towards Heinrich.

293   THREE SHOT FEATURING HEINRICH (SAM, ROMEO)

Heinrich is watching Parker with the partisans; he has a little worried frown on his forehead; he runs the tip of his tongue over his lips in a small gesture of apprehension.

294   LONG SHOT   PARKER AND PARTISANS   POV HEINRICH

Volpe seems almost angrily agitated; he gestures towards Heinrich; Parker shakes his head - but without any real conviction.

295   CLOSE SHOT   HEINRICH

He is trying to make out what the men are talking about - to no avail; he looks concerned.

296   LONG SHOT   PARKER AND PARTISANS   PAN

With a final negative gesture Parker leaves the men, who scowl grimly after him, as he walks back to Heinrich and his guards. CAMERA PANS him to a MED. GROUP SHOT.

> PARKER
> Okay - come on!

They start away - walking into a small street leading off the village square.

EXT. DESERTED SPOT BEHIND FARM HOUSE   DAWN

297   WIDE SHOT

Parker, Heinrich and his guards come into the farm yard; they walk to the farm house. Parker grabs a spade leaning against the wall; deliberately he measures out a rectangle in the dirt - six by two feet.

(CONTINUED)

97.

297 CONTINUED:

Then he throws the spade at Heinrich, who manages just to get his hands down in time to catch it, before it slams into him.

      PARKER
 Dig!

Heinrich looks at the three men incredulously. Sam and Romeo lower their rifles at him menacingly.

      PARKER
 Dig!

And Heinrich digs - tensely, grimly contemplating the ultimate use of the suggestive excavation.

298 CLOSE SHOT HEINRICH

Soberly he is digging.

299 CLOSE SHOT PARKER

Granite-faced he is watching the German.

300 TWO SHOT ROMEO, SAM

They are watching the prisoner - stony-faced.

301 MED. GROUP SHOT DOLLY IN

Watched by his guards Heinrich is laboring at the excavation, which is rapidly taking shape. A small mound of dirt is forming to one side of it. CAMERA DOLLIES IN to a CLOSE SHOT of the little mound of dirt - as each new spadeful makes it a little bigger...

      CUT TO:

302 CLOSE SHOT DIRT MOUND DOLLY OUT

The dirt heap has grown considerably; CAMERA DOLLIES OUT to a MED. SHOT. Heinrich is standing in the bottom of the rectangular excavation, which is now about two feet deep; he is sweating - working along. The three others are watching him.

      PARKER
 Okay - that's enough. Get out!

      (CONTINUED)

302 CONTINUED:

Heinrich throws the spade on the dirt heap and climbs out; he stands at the end of the hole - facing Parker...Slowly Parker draws his '45; he glares at the German.

> PARKER
> Now, Lieutenant Heinrich, talk! Or you may never have a chance to talk again!

303 CLOSE SHOT HEINRICH

His sweaty face is dirty; the muscles of his jaw cord - but he remains silent.

304 CLOSE SHOT   PARKER

His eyes are terrible, as they seem to bore into the prisoner.

305 TWO SHOT

Without another word Parker cocks his gun; the metallic CLICK is loud in the strained silence; Heinrich stands even more erect, but his eyes give the tiniest flicker towards the ominously gaping grave directly in back of him.

> PARKER
> I advise you not to be stubborn, Lieutenant.

Heinrich remains silent.

> PARKER
> You have nothing to say?

Heinrich does not make a sound - or move...Slowly Parker raises his gun to point straight at the German...

> HEINRICH
> (suddenly)
> Yes! Yes - I have something to say!

Parker gives an almost imperceptible sigh of relief.

> PARKER
> Then talk!

> HEINRICH
> I shall talk, Captain...But only to tell you that not for one moment do I believe you will shoot me in cold blood! I am a prisoner of war.

(CONTINUED)

305 CONTINUED:

Parker bites down hard to control himself; then - with icy calm:

          PARKER
You are that certain?

          HEINRICH
I am. It is not the way of an officer in the American Army.

          PARKER
Why not? It *is* the way of officers in the German Army! Or haven't you heard of Malmedy!?

          HEINRICH
I have. It is to be regretted. But we are not all like that.

306 CLOSE SHOT   PARKER

He is glaring at the German officer with dark, frustrated fury.

307 CLOSE SHOT   HEINRICH

He is meeting Parker's look straight on.

          HEINRICH
If you kill me, Captain, then you are no better than the *worst* of us!

308 TWO SHOT

The two men stand face to face for a moment, glaring at each other; then Parker lowers his gun.

          PARKER
You are right, Lieutenant. I have no desire to sink to that level. Fortunately I don't have to!

309 MED. SHOT

Parker turns to Sam brusquely.

          PARKER
Sam!

At once Sam hurries off - leaving the others behind...Not a word is spoken. In the far distance the staccato bark of a machine gun can be heard.

310 CLOSE SHOT   HEINRICH

He is getting the tiniest worried frown on his forehead.

311 CLOSE SHOT   PARKER

He looks stony.

312 MED. SHOT

The men are looking tensely at one another...Suddenly Sam comes around the farm house corner - but he is not alone. Volpe, Tony and a few of the other partisans are with him. The men look towards the approaching group.

313 CLOSE SHOT   HEINRICH

He grows pale at the sight of the fierce looking partisans; his eyes widen.

314 GROUP SHOT   PARTISANS

Scowling menacingly they advance on the tableau; CAMERA CARRIES them to a MED. GROUP SHOT. The partisans stop in front of Heinrich; they look a frightening lot.

315 TWO SHOT   PARKER, HEINRICH

       PARKER
      (grimly)
  Well, Lieutenant...Shall we have our
  little talk - or shall I leave you to
  these gentlemen - who may not have as
  many scruples as I do?

Heinrich's eyes flick towards the menace of Volpe and his men.

       HEINRICH
  I shall give you no information,
  Captain.

       PARKER
  You've made your choice, then...

316 MED. SHOT

       PARKER
     (to Romeo and Sam)
  Come on!

(CONTINUED)

316   CONTINUED:

He starts away; the partisans begin to close in on Heinrich.

>   HEINRICH
> Captain!

Parker stops - but he doesn't turn towards Heinrich.

>   HEINRICH
> You cannot wash responsibility from
> your hands! It was tried once before
> - in vain!

For a long moment Parker and the others stand immobile...
Then Parker seems to sag a little.

>   PARKER
>   (quietly)
> Take him back!

Sam and Romeo at once move to obey. They start to lead
Heinrich off...Heinrich stops and turns toward Parker.

>   HEINRICH
> Captain, according to the Geneva
> Conventions a Prisoner of War must
> be evacuated from the front to a
> safe spot. I respectfully enquire
> when I shall be evacuated?

317   CLOSEUP   PARKER

He reacts; but he does not answer.

318   MED. SHOT

Sam and Romeo prod Heinrich along; Volpe steps up to Parker.

319   TWO SHOT   VOLPE, PARKER

>   VOLPE
> Leave him with us!
>
>   PARKER
> No.
>
>   VOLPE
> We'll make him talk!
>
>   PARKER
>   (vehemently)
> No!

(CONTINUED)

319   CONTINUED:

Volpe shrugs elaborately; he spits in the grave - and turns to leave.

320   MED. SHOT

Sam and Romeo are disappearing around the farm house with their prisoner; the partisans walk off in the other direction - leaving Parker alone...CAMERA DOLLIES IN to a CLOSE SHOT of Parker, as he looks after the departing Heinrich with a puzzled, pensive frown.

321   WIDER ANGLE

Parker turns to look at the open slit trench dug by the prisoner. In the b.g. around the corner of the farm house come Sgt. Hicks and Alvin; Alvin carries a fence pole and Sgt. Hicks a board of wood; purposefully they march up to Parker and the slit trench.

> HICKS
> (briskly - to Alvin)
> Okay, Alvin - do your stuff...

Alvin proceeds to plant the fence pole firmly in the mound of dirt, as Hicks turns to Parker.

> HICKS
> (cheerfully)
> Should have thought of this little trick long ago, sir. Even when it doesn't work for you, it sure comes in handy for us!

He turns to the pole - and with a flourish he hangs the sign board on the pole.

322   CLOSE SHOT   SIGN ON POLE

In big, bold letters it reads:

L A T R I N E

MATCH CUT TO:

INT. S-2 ROOM OF SANTA MARIA SCHOOL HOUSE   AFTERNOON

323   CLOSE SHOT   SIGN ON DOOR

It reads:
R E G I M E N T A L   S - 2
Major Paul Armstrong

(CONTINUED)

323   CONTINUED:

The door opens, as a G.I. comes out of the room; CAMERA DOLLIES IN through the open door. There are three men in the room; Colonel Bradford, Captain Parker and Major Armstrong - who is talking - and whom CAMERA FAVORS.

> ARMSTRONG
> (overbearing)
> Let's face it, Parker, you're getting nowhere!

> PARKER
> Lieutenant Heinrich is not an ordinary PW. He's not easy to break...

> ARMSTRONG
> Dammit, Captain, we want results - not excuses!

Armstrong turns to Bradford.

> ARMSTRONG
> (strongly)
> Sir, I must insist it's time for stronger measures! Obviously, Heinrich's not going to fall for any of Captain Parker's childish tricks! He won't talk - simply because he doesn't believe himself to be in any real danger. I say - show him otherwise!

324   TWO SHOT   PARKER, ARMSTRONG

> PARKER
> (white-faced)
> You want me to use force! You want me to deal with them on their level!

> ARMSTRONG
> I want information!

> PARKER
> And you want me to get it by doing exactly the same they do - by being just as rotten as they are!

> ARMSTRONG
> Yes, man! If necessary - yes!

> PARKER
> Then what are we fighting for?!

(CONTINUED)

324 CONTINUED:

                    ARMSTRONG
        I don't give a damn how you get
        the information. Just get it!

325 THREE SHOT

Parker, tight-lipped, turns to Bradford.

                    PARKER
        Sir, am I to understand that my
        interrogation methods from now on
        are to be dictated by Major
        Armstrong?

Bradford looks at Parker seriously.

                    BRADFORD
        Does he have a point?

Parker looks haunted. Perhaps Armstrong *is* right...But Parker is not yet ready to surrender his *convictions*; he does not reply.

                    BRADFORD
        Can you get the information we need,
        in time?

                    PARKER
        Violence won't do it, sir. I'll
        stake my life on that!

                    BRADFORD
        <u>Can you get it</u>?

326 CLOSE SHOT   PARKER

After a pause:

                    PARKER
        Yes, sir. I can.

                  ARMSTRONG (o.s.)
        You're sticking your neck out,
        Parker...Way out!

                    PARKER
        I know.

327 CLOSE SHOT   BRADFORD

He makes up his mind.

                                        (CONTINUED)

327   CONTINUED:

                    BRADFORD
          Alright...He's your baby, Dirk.
          Make him sing!

328   MED. SHOT

                    PARKER
          Yes, sir! Thank you.

He salutes and leaves the room. CAMERA DOLLIES IN to a
CLOSE TWO SHOT. Bradford looks after Parker with a grave,
speculative expression - Armstrong glowers angrily.

EXT. SANTA MARIA FARM YARD   DAY

329   MED. SHOT   SAM   PAN SHOT

He is walking guard in front of a house; he carries his gun
at port arms...CAMERA PANS him, as he walks back and forth -
obviously on the alert...CAMERA PULLS BACK to reveal a man
quietly coming up behind Sam. It is Volpe. Suddenly Sam
hears him - he whirls on the man - pointing the gun at him.

                    SAM
          Hold it! Hold it right there!

Volpe grins; he holds his hands up nonchalantly; he is
unarmed.

                    VOLPE
          Okay, soldier, okay!

                    SAM
          Turn around! Keep your hands up!

With a shrug Volpe lazily obeys...Sam carefully walks up
behind him. Suddenly Volpe flies into action; he twists,
ducks and deals a numbing blow to Sam's arm - all in one
movement; and before one can really see how it's done -
Volpe stands with Sam's gun in his hand - pointed straight
at the dazed, surprised soldier sitting on the ground.
(NOTE: The action will be staged to show the actual
demonstration of disarming an enemy, as taught in Commando
Schools.)

CAMERA PULLS BACK FURTHER, as Sgt. Hicks walks up to the
open-mouthed Sam, still sitting on the ground.

                    HICKS
          Okay, Sam, get your butt up!

                              (CONTINUED)

106.

329　CONTINUED:

Sam gets to his feet, looking sheepish, as Hicks reaches for the gun held by Volpe, who gives it to him. Hicks turns, as CAMERA PULLS STILL FURTHER OUT to reveal a group of G.I.'s sitting in a semi-circle in front of Volpe and Hicks.

>   HICKS
>   That's how it's done!

330　GROUP SHOT　SOLDIERS

In the front row sit Alvin and Pinto; Alvin looks properly impressed.

>   HICKS (o.s.)
>   Now let's see if you've learned
>   anything...Alvin! Front and center!

Alvin gets up, and CAMERA CARRIES him, as he walks over to Hicks. Hicks gives him the rifle.

>   HICKS
>   Okay. Now - if you were on guard
>   and saw an enemy soldier coming
>   towards you - what would you do?

Alvin looks thoughtful; he regards the gun in his hands seriously - then he holds it out.

>   ALVIN
>   Well, Sarge, the first thing I'd
>   do is to get rid of this thing -
>   before he could take it away from
>   me and kill me with it!

The G.I.'s howl; Hicks himself has trouble keeping from laughing.

>   HICKS
>   Alvin, you'll never know your
>   assault from a hole in the ground!

The scene is cut short by Parker's arrival. The Captain walks up to Hicks.

>   PARKER
>   Hicks, get Heinrich. Bring him
>   to the IPW room. We'll have one
>   more try...

>   HICKS
>   Yes, sir. I'll have him there at
>   once!

INT. IPW ROOM OF SANTA MARIA SCHOOL HOUSE   DAY

331   MED. CLOSEUP   HEINRICH

He is standing in front of Parker's desk. Outside can be heard the rumble of heavy vehicles, as the first elements of Corps Forward are arriving in the village.

CAMERA WIDENS to reveal Parker seated at his desk facing the German.

> PARKER
> It makes no sense, Heinrich. Why prolong a war that is already lost?

> HEINRICH
> The war goes on.

> PARKER
> Even your own High Command knows, you've lost the war. That's why they tried to do away with Hitler.

> HEINRICH
> A small group of traitors!

> PARKER
> The day will come, when you'll realize, they were patriots.

> HEINRICH
> Never!

> PARKER
> Don't be too sure.

> HEINRICH
> I have my convictions, sir.

> PARKER
> A man with firm convictions, Heinrich, can so easily become pig-headed!

> HEINRICH
> Captain, may I ask you a question?

> PARKER
> Go ahead.

> HEINRICH
> If you were in my position, would you give information?

Parker does not answer, but it is obvious, what the answer would be.

(CONTINUED)

331 CONTINUED:

>   HEINRICH
>   (quietly)
>   What makes you think that I am less
>   honorable than you?

The two men look firmly at one another.

332 CLOSE SHOT   FACE OF GRANDFATHER CLOCK

It shows a few minutes past five o'clock. CAMERA PANS DOWN to a CLOSE SHOT of the pendulum; it is swinging back and forth rhythmically; CAMERA PANS BACK UP to a CLOSE SHOT of the clock face; it is now about twenty minutes before ten o'clock.

>   PARKER (o.s.)
>   ...the Polish Campaign was a long
>   time ago, Lieutenant.

333 TWO SHOT   PARKER, HEINRICH

>   PARKER
>   (continues)
>   Where have you been fighting since
>   then?
>
>   HEINRICH
>   I cannot say, sir.

Both men look tired, their voices are weary. The lamp in the room is burning brightly; the blackout curtains are closed.

>   PARKER
>   Heinrich, you're an idiot! Don't
>   you realize that if you don't talk
>   to me, I'll have to turn you over
>   to another interrogator?
>
>   HEINRICH
>   Yes, sir...
>
>   PARKER
>   (sternly)
>   That means Captain Goldstein,
>   Lieutenant! Captain Solomon
>   Goldstein! Of Polish descent! His
>   parents died in Warsaw. In the
>   Ghetto! You want _him_ to take over?!

Heinrich looks nervous; he glances towards the clock.

(CONTINUED)

333 CONTINUED:

>   HEINRICH
> I can give no information, sir.

Parker studies the man before him; then he suddenly changes his attitude.

>   PARKER
>   (quietly)
> Alright, Lieutenant Heinrich. Let's
> call it a day, what do you say?
> Think it over - and get a good night's
> rest.

Heinrich looks even more nervous; he glances again towards the clock; he wets his lips.

>   HEINRICH
>   (tensely)
> Captain, I respectfully request that
> I be evacuated to an area behind the
> front...

Parker looks at the man; he notices his apparent nervousness; a small puzzled frown passes over his face - but he is too tired to see the real significance behind the German's request.

>   PARKER
>   (wearily)
> Sergeant Hicks!

334 WIDER ANGLE

Hicks at the door snaps to.

>   HICKS
> Sir?

>   PARKER
> Take him away.

Hicks opens the door and calls.

>   HICKS
> Guards!

Alvin and Pinto enter; Heinrich clicks his heels - and follows them towards the door; he hesitates at the door - is just about to speak, but changes his mind. Alvin and Pinto take him out; Hicks goes over to Parker. CAMERA DOLLIES IN to a CLOSE TWO SHOT.

(CONTINUED)

334 CONTINUED:

>   HICKS
>   What a stubborn mule. Good thing
>   they aren't all like that.
>
>   PARKER
>   I can't make him out...Something's
>   bugging him - I'm sure of it...
>   Something I'm missing...
>
>   HICKS
>   And we went almost through our
>   entire list of bluffs.
>
>   PARKER
>   What's worse - he knows we're
>   bluffing...
>   (different thought)
>   I have a hunch he'll break, Hicks...
>
>   HICKS
>   Yeah. He does seem wound up like
>   a mainspring.
>
>   PARKER
>   I need a smoke - and a couple of
>   hours' rest. We'll trot him out
>   again in a little while...let's say
>   in three hours.
>
>   HICKS
>   (concerned)
>   You won't get much sleep, sir.
>   Easy does it!
>
>   PARKER
>   Sure. But when easy does it -
>   somebody usually has to do it over
>   again. You putting in for the job?
>
>   HICKS
>   Not me, sir! I never --
>
>   PARKER & HICKS
>   (in unison)
>   ...volunteered for anything since
>   basic training!

Parker grins.

>   PARKER
>   I know! -- Grab some bunk fatigue
>   yourself...

(CONTINUED)

334   CONTINUED: - 2

> HICKS
> Yes, sir. And, sir?...What does one have to do to get out of this chicken outfit?!

Parker grins.

> PARKER
> Drop dead!

He leaves.

335   CLOSE SHOT   HICKS

He looks after the IPW with genuine concern.

EXT. SANTA MARIA VILLAGE SQUARE   NIGHT

336   WIDE SHOT FEATURING FOUNTAIN

The place is milling with personnel and equipment as Corps Forward is taking over. Parker is making his way to the fountain.

337   CLOSER ANGLE

Parker stops and leans against the founatin; he takes a deep breath of air - and begins to fish out a cigarette. Sam and Romeo pass by.

> ROMEO
> ...so I figured after six hours on - dragging my arsenal all over hell's half acre, I'm entitled to a little hot chow. And what d'ya think they got?

> SAM
> Let me guess...Sh -- on the shingles!

A jeep roars its motor just at the crucial moment, drowning out the first word - and the first word only - of the well known army dish! Sam and Romeo walk off.

338   CLOSE SHOT   PARKER

He is lighting his cigarette. Suddenly Rina's voice is heard o.s.

(CONTINUED)

338 CONTINUED:

> RINA
> You play hooky from the school?

339 WIDER ANGLE

Rina stands next to Parker; she again is clad in her combat outfit; she carries a German Schmeisser machine pistol; she is ready to go.

> PARKER
> Rina!

He notices her dress and the gun; his face clouds over.

> PARKER
> You're going with Volpe.

> RINA
> (she nods; soberly)
> We are leaving soon...

Parker looks unhappy.

> RINA
> I told you. I have a debt to pay...

Parker nods at the gun.

> PARKER
> With that?

Rina does not answer.

> PARKER
> I guess you must do what you think is right...

> RINA
> So must you!

They look earnestly at one another; then Rina breaks the solemn mood; her eyes twinkle - she seems somehow changed; softer - warmer - more feminine, even with the gun in her hand - as she looks with concern into Parker's troubled face.

> RINA
> You will not forget me?

> PARKER
> You can bet on that! Even if I have to remember you as a bloodthirsty partisan!

(CONTINUED)

339   CONTINUED:

>   RINA
>   I tell you how I was before...Once
>   my uncle ask me to kill a chicken.
>   I could not do it!
>
>   PARKER
>   But now - you think nothing of
>   killing a German...
>
>   RINA
>   (with a mischievous
>   smile)
>   The chicken did not say, "Heil
>   Hitler!"

She looks affectionately at Parker.

>   RINA
>   But - I think I kill no more
>   Germans - now..!
>
>   PARKER
>   Good!

He stands close to her; they are oblivious of all the activity around them.

>   PARKER
>   (earnestly)
>   Take care...

Without taking her eyes from him Rina nods solemnly ...
A truck roars by - momentarily obliterating the scene...
When it passes, a new scene is revealed -

INT. STORE ROOM CELL   NIGHT

340   MED. SHOT

Heinrich is walking up and down in his little ground floor store room cell; he acts extremely nervous and apprehensive; he keeps looking at his watch. Suddenly he makes up his mind; he strides to the door and begins to bang on it.

>   HEINRICH
>   Guard!

INT. CORRIDOR   NIGHT

341   MED. SHOT ALVIN

He is standing guard; he is leaning against the wall - rifle in hand; startled he jumps at the sudden commotion.

(CONTINUED)

114.

341 CONTINUED:

Heinrich's voice is heard from the cell:

> HEINRICH
> Guard!...Guard!

> ALVIN
> (calling)
> Hey - take it easy, will'ya?

He starts toward the door - then he stops...Thoughtfully he looks at the rifle in his hands - then he leans it against the wall out of the way, and goes over to the cell door. He starts to open it, but thinks better of it.

342 CLOSE SHOT   ALVIN

at the door.

> ALVIN
> Okay, okay. Don't get your beans in an uproar! What do you want?

INT. STORE ROOM CELL   NIGHT

343   CLOSE SHOT   HEINRICH

His head is close to the door.

> HEINRICH
> I want to see the Captain. Captain Parker!

INT. CORRIDOR   NIGHT

344   CLOSE SHOT   ALVIN

> ALVIN
> You nuts? It's late...

> HEINRICH (o.s.)
> I know it is late!

INT. STORE ROOM CELL   NIGHT

345   CLOSE SHOT   HEINRICH

> HEINRICH
> (continues)
> I must see him. At once! It is very urgent!

INT. CORRIDOR   NIGHT

346   MED. SHOT   ALVIN

He thinks for a moment.

                HEINRICH (o.s.)
Guard!

                ALVIN
Simmer down! I'll find out if <u>he</u>
wants to see <u>you</u>!

INT. STORE ROOM CELL   NIGHT

347   MED. CLOSE SHOT   HEINRICH

                HEINRICH
He must! You hear - he <u>must</u>!

He listens for a moment; there is no answer.

                HEINRICH
Guard!

Still no answer. Heinrich bangs his fist against the door in frustration; he looks around his cell like a desperate, caged animal.

INT. IPW ROOM IN SANTA MARIA SCHOOL HOUSE   NIGHT

348   MED. CLOSE SHOT   PARKER

He is sleeping on his cot - fully clothed; a hand comes into the picture and gently shakes him; almost at once Parker sits up - wide awake. CAMERA PULLS BACK to reveal Hicks.

                HICKS
Sorry to wake you, Sir. But that
Kraut - Heinrich - he's yelling
bloody murder. Wants to see you...

Parker sits up at the edge of the cot.

                PARKER
He does, does he? What time is it?

                HICKS
            (glancing at the
            big clock)
Not quite half past ten.

                PARKER
Hicks...I knew <u>something</u> was eating
that guy.

                      (CONTINUED)

348   CONTINUED:

He stands up, goes to his desk, picks out some papers and lights a cigarette, during:

> PARKER
> Okay. We're in the driver's seat now. Let's make sure we stay there.

> HICKS
> Right.

> PARKER
> We'll ignore him - for now...

> HICKS
> He'll howl! Says it's just about the most important thing in the whole lousy war that he gets to talk to you.

> PARKER
> Quite a switch...We'll let him stew for a while...At eleven o'clock - bring him up.

> HICKS
> Okay. Eleven it is.

He leaves.

INT. CORRIDOR   NIGHT

349   MED. SHOT

Alvin is on guard. Hicks comes in.

> ALVIN
> We get him?

Hicks shakes his head.

> HICKS
> (softly)
> Wear him down a bit...

CAMERA CARRIES him, as he walks to a torn, stuffed easy chair standing in the corridor before a couple of packing crates forming a table. He looks relaxed; he yawns and sits down comfortably in the chair.

350   CLOSE SHOT   HICKS

He takes off his watch - looks at it, opens the case with a little knife and studies the inside.

351 CLOSEUP   WATCH MOVEMENT (STOCK)

352 CLOSE SHOT   HICKS

With knowing hands he adjusts the movement; then he takes three more watches from his pocket.

353 CLOSE SHOT   FOUR WATCHES

They all show exactly 10:47.

INT. STORE ROOM CELL   NIGHT

354 MED. CLOSE SHOT   HEINRICH

He is looking at his watch; his tenseness is increasing; he paces up and down - always hesitating in front of the door; he walks toward it, as if intending to knock on it - but changes his mind.

INT. CORRIDOR   NIGHT

355 MED. CLOSE SHOT   HICKS

In contrast to Heinrich he is very much at ease; he straps on his own watch and looks approvingly at the other three watches before putting them back in his pocket...Then he looks at the time on his wrist watch.

356 CLOSEUP   WRIST WATCH

It shows 10:53.

357 MED. SHOT   HICKS

He leans back in the chair and puts his feet up on the crate table...Suddenly we HEAR a loud POUNDING on the cell door. Hicks reacts.

INT. STORE ROOM CELL   NIGHT

358 MED. CLOSE SHOT   HEINRICH

He is pounding on the door; he looks very worried.

                        HEINRICH
            Guard! Guard!

118.

INT. CORRIDOR   NIGHT

359   MED. SHOT

Hicks goes to the door; he motions to Alvin to open up; Alvin does. At once Heinrich appears in the open door; he looks and acts agitated.

>   HICKS
> What's all the racket? Take it easy!
>
>   HEINRICH
> I demand to see the Captain! At once!
>
>   HICKS
> Demand!? Well - well - well..!
>
>   HEINRICH
> It's a matter of life or death!
>
>   HICKS
> Really?

With maddening slowness and deliberation he takes out his three watches and studies each in turn, while Heinrich looks on in frustrated impatience. Finally Hicks looks at the watch on his wrist.

>   HICKS
> Well...I guess the Captain is about ready for you now...

INT. IPW ROOM OF SANTA MARIA SCHOOL HOUSE   NIGHT

360   MED. CLOSE SHOT   PARKER

He is working at his desk; he stops - and stretches. Then he walks over to one of the school desks; he places his steel helmet, bowl fashion, on it and pours water into it from his canteen. Then he dips his hands in it - and vigorously rubs his face with the cool water...CAMERA DOLLIES IN to a HIGH, CLOSE SHOT of the ROUND HELMET; the light from the ceiling bulb is shimmering in the agitated water...

                                        MATCH CUT TO:

361   CLOSE SHOT   THE ROUND FACE OF THE GRANDFATHER CLOCK

It shows 11:00 o'clock; it starts to chime...

362 WIDER ANGLE

Parker goes to sit at his desk; he is relaxed and rested; there is a KNOCK on the door; at once Parker makes himself look very busy with some papers on his desk - then he snaps:

          PARKER
Come in!

The door opens and Hicks marches in with the excited looking Heinrich. The clock stops chiming. Parker does not look up from his work, as Heinrich stands at attention before him. A long moment goes by; Heinrich looks impatiently "fidgety" ...At last Parker says - still without looking up:

          PARKER
        (disinterested)
Alright, Lieutenant Heinrich. You wanted to see me?

          HEINRICH
        (formally)
I want to make a statement.

          PARKER
Go ahead.

          HEINRICH
There is no time to waste, Captain. You must understand, why I am doing this...

Parker looks up at him sharply.

          HEINRICH
        (continues)
I want to save lives! Your lives! American lives!

          PARKER
        (sharply)
What is it?

          HEINRICH
My battery of 88's have been given a fire mission, sir. Santa Maria!

          PARKER
We always get some shells...

          HEINRICH
This is different.

          PARKER
Oh?

                    (CONTINUED)

362   CONTINUED:

> HEINRICH
> (urgently)
> We know you plan an offensive!
> We know Santa Maria will be the
> center of it!

Parker reacts to this.

> PARKER
>
> Go on!

> HEINRICH
>
> This fire mission is a concentrated
> barrage! Santa Maria will be razed
> to the ground! Every building in it
> destroyed! We are zeroed in on the
> school house!

> PARKER
>
> When?

> HEINRICH
>
> Midnight!

> PARKER
> (to Hicks)
> Hicks! Get Bradford! On the double!

Hicks at once hurries from the room.

> HEINRICH
> (rationalizing)
> It makes no difference I tell you
> this. The barrage can not be stopped.
> My capture will not affect it. Santa
> Maria will be destroyed. The offensive
> will be stopped!

> PARKER
>
> You are the battery observer?

> HEINRICH
> (proudly)
> I am.

He glances at the clock.

> HEINRICH
>
> There is less than an hour, Captain.
> We must get out of Santa Maria.

> PARKER
>
> Where is the location of your battery?

(CONTINUED)

362   CONTINUED: - 2

Heinrich looks at him with a thin smile.

                HEINRICH
Sorry, Captain!

The door bursts open and Bradford comes hurrying in, followed by Hicks. Bradford makes straight for Parker.

363   TWO SHOT   BRADFORD, PARKER

The two men talk in low, tense voices.

                BRADFORD
What's this about a maximum effort barrage on Santa Maria?

                PARKER
             (he nods
              emphatically)
At midnight, sir! This building is the zero point.

                BRADFORD
             (with a nod towards
              Heinrich)
He told you?

                PARKER
Yes, sir.

                BRADFORD
             (with a frown)
He could be handing you a line, Dirk. A trick to make us evacuate the village...

                PARKER
No, sir. I'm sure he's telling the truth.

                BRADFORD
             (sharply)
Why?

                PARKER
All through his interrogation I've felt there was something - strange - about him. I figured I'd find out - given a little time. This is it! He wanted to get out of Santa Maria the worst way! Now we know why! I'm certain he's on the level!

122.

364 CLOSE SHOT   BRADFORD

He looks closely at Parker.

> BRADFORD
> I'll give the order to evacuate at once!

365 WIDER ANGLE

Hicks, having overheard the Colonel, hurries from the room.

366 CLOSE SHOT   BRADFORD

He looks seriously at Parker.

> BRADFORD
> And, Dirk...Get us the location of that damned battery! We can get the troops out of here alright - but if Santa Maria is blasted to hell - it would foul up the whole offensive!

367 CLOSE SHOT PARKER

> PARKER
> (gravely)
> I'll get it for you, sir.

He glances towards the big clock.

368 CLOSE SHOT   CLOCK

It shows 11:13.

369 TWO SHOT   BRADFORD, PARKER

Bradford looks searchingly at Parker.

> BRADFORD
> I'll alert artillery for counter battery action. Use the field phone. We'll keep the line open.. Good luck!

370 WIDER ANGLE

Bradford hurries from the room, as Hicks enters with Alvin, Pinto and Romeo.

(CONTINUED)

370   CONTINUED:

                    HICKS
                (directing the men)
You take that file there...Grab those bags...that stuff over there. Shake it up!

The men get busy; Hicks himself goes for the map on the blackboard.

                    PARKER
Leave the map here!

Hicks looks at Parker in astonishment. The G.I.'s hurry from the room with the various items. Hicks goes over to Parker.

371   TWO SHOT   PARKER, HICKS

Parker looks darkly at him; he does not answer; he draws his '45 and places himself with the desk between himself and Heinrich - facing the grave German officer.

                    HICKS
                (grimly)
Major Armstrong's methods, sir?

                    PARKER
                (with quiet authority)
Sergeant Hicks, take the gun - and the Thompson. And get out of here!

                    HICKS
                (startled)
But - sir!...

                    PARKER
                (sharply)
Go on!

Without another word Hicks obeys. He leaves...Parker and Heinrich are left alone in the doomed school house of little Santa Maria village..! Heinrich looks toward the door - then he begins to move towards it.

                    PARKER
We're not going anywhere, Lieutenant!

                    HEINRICH
                (taken aback)
But - in a few minutes...the barrage! This place will be a death trap!

                            (CONTINUED)

371 CONTINUED:

>   PARKER
>   Perhaps...Unless we silence the
>   battery first!
>
>   HEINRICH
>   (beginning to lose
>   his self-assurance)
>   Keeping me here is in violation of
>   the Geneva Convention.
>
>   PARKER
>   Your frequently quoted Geneva
>   Conventions states that a PW must
>   be given the same protection as an
>   American soldier...

372 CLOSEUP   PARKER

>   PARKER
>   (continues)
>   I am an American soldier!

373 CLOSEUP   HEINRICH

He reacts - as Parker's intentions sink in.

374 MED. SHOT

The very air in the room is charged and tense...The ticking of the big grandfather clock seems louder than usual. Slowly - never taking his eyes off Heinrich - Parker goes over to the clock; it shows 11:27. He reaches for the swinging pendulum - and stops it! The ticking at once falls silent - the clock goes dead...The sudden silence is thunderous!

375 CLOSE SHOT   HEINRICH

With a worried frown he watches Parker.

376 CLOSE SHOT   PARKER   PAN

CAMERA CARRIES Parker, as he returns to his desk and sits down. WIDEN to a TWO SHOT. Deliberately Parker takes off his watch and puts it on the desk.

>   PARKER
>   (curtly)
>   Take off your watch!

(CONTINUED)

376   CONTINUED:

Heinrich obeys.

> PARKER
> Throw it over here!

Reluctantly Heinrich does as he is told - and Parker places both watches in the desk drawer, out of sight...From outside the hectic sounds and noises of the hurried evacuation drift into the quiet school room.

377   CLOSE SHOT PARKER

Grimly, stony-faced he is watching the German in his battle of nerves.

378   CLOSE SHOT HEINRICH

He tries to wet his lips...This time the American is not just bluffing; this time the danger is real. Death is inevitable - unless...He grimaces a tortured query at Parker.

379   CLOSE SHOT PARKER

> PARKER
> No, Lieutenant...This time I'm not bluffing!

380   CLOSE SHOT HEINRICH

> HEINRICH
> There is not much time...

381   TWO SHOT

> PARKER
> (relentlessly)
> Where is the battery position, Lieutenant? Where?!

Heinrich bites his lips; the muscles cord in his jaw; his eyes are drawn irresistibly to the immobile clock face... time seems eternal.

> HEINRICH
> This is madness! We will both be killed!

> PARKER
> It's up to you. There's still time.

(CONTINUED)

381 CONTINUED:

>   HEINRICH
> You - want to die?!
>
>   PARKER
>   (quiet conviction)
> There are more important things
> than that. You see - I believe in
> what I'm fighting for - That's our
> real "secret weapon!"

382 CLOSE SHOT   HEINRICH

He reacts sharply to this statement; a shadow of defeat begins to creep into his eyes. He looks towards the silent, dead clock.

383 CLOSEUP CLOCK FACE

It is quiet - the hands are motionless - frozen at 11:27.

                                        MATCH CUT TO:

EXT. 88 BATTERY POSITION   NIGHT

384 CLOSE SHOT   88 MM GUN MUZZLE (STOCK)

The black,,gaping roundness of the 88mm gun muzzle fills the SCREEN. The gun is being placed in position.

385 WIDER SHOT (STOCK)

We see the activity of the gun battery getting ready for a big fire mission. The location is a rocky mountain ledge near a large cave.

386 MED. CLOSE SHOT   SCHILLER

He is directing the activity.

387 OTHER ACTIVITY SHOTS OF AN 88 GUN BATTERY   (STOCK)

as above.

388 CLOSE SHOT   88 GUN (STOCK)

The gun is ready to fire.

                                        MATCH CUT TO:

INT. IPW ROOM OF SANTA MARIA SCHOOL HOUSE   NIGHT

389   CLOSE SHOT '45

Held in Parker's hand - it is aimed at Heinrich - ready to fire. CAMERA PULLS OUT to a TWO SHOT of Parker and Heinrich. The waiting in the school house is becoming almost unbearable. A lone motor is HEARD RACING in the distance outside - then everything is deadly quiet...How much time left? Minutes?...Seconds??

390   CLOSE SHOT HEINRICH

Little beads of moisture are forming on the man's brow; a tiny artery in his temple beats and beats and beats...

391   CLOSE SHOT PARKER

He is granite-faced; only a superhuman effort keeps him from looking at the watch in the desk drawer...But Heinrich must not be allowed to read in his face, how much time is left - before...

392   TWO SHOT

                    HEINRICH
          I told the truth. I was not
          bluffing! I myself registered the
          fire...

                    PARKER
          Good. Then you know where the
          battery is!

                    HEINRICH
          It - it might start any minute!

                    PARKER
          Any second...

Heinrich looks panic-stricken.

                    HEINRICH
          I must get out!

He starts for the door; Parker at once jumps to his feet - gun aimed at Heinrich.

                    PARKER
          Hold it!

(CONTINUED)

392 CONTINUED:

Heinrich stops; he is breathing heavily. For a moment the two men stand tensely, glaring at one another...Then Heinrich looks towards the silent clock...he seems to sag; his face falls tired and dead...

                    HEINRICH
          Alright. I show you.

At once Parker motions him to the blackboard map.

                    PARKER
          Over there!

Heinrich starts for the map. As he passes Parker he leaps for him. But Parker is ready for him; a quick rabbit punch sends the German sprawling...When he gets to his feet, he again finds himself facing Parker's drawn '45. Darkly the IPW says:

                    PARKER
          This time I'll use it! Now - where
          is that battery position?

Heinrich glances at the frozen clock; he looks back at Parker.

                    HEINRICH
          How - much time?

                    PARKER
          The guns?!

Heinrich walks to the map; he studies it.

                    HEINRICH
          This map is - different ... different
          from ours...
                    (he searches desperately)
          Here!
                    (he points)
          Here - on this shelf. There is the
          battery.

                    PARKER
          There are no guns there! We've
          checked by air!

                    HEINRICH
                    (almost pleadingly)
          They're there, Captain! During the
          day they are pulled into a big cave.
          You cannot see them...They'll be out
          now!

                                        (CONTINUED)

129.

392   CONTINUED: - 2

    Parker reacts to this information. Then he quickly looks at the map; he strides to the field phone.

393   CLOSE SHOT   PARKER

on the phone.

                    PARKER
                 (urgently)
    Retread Three!...Here's your target.
    Coordinates: 4 - 8 - 7 and 5 - 3 - 1
    ...Hurry!

He turns to Heinrich.

                    PARKER
    You'd better be right!

394   TWO SHOT

                    HEINRICH
    We must hurry! We must take cover.

He turns towards the door. Parker stops him.

                    PARKER
    Stay here!

Heinrich stops; he looks at Parker incredulously.

                    HEINRICH
    I told you where the guns are!
    Now we must get out of here!

                    PARKER
                 (firmly)
    No!

395   CLOSE SHOT   HEINRICH

He looks thunderstruck.

396   CLOSE SHOT   PARKER

A thin, mirthless smile plays over his lips.

                    PARKER
    You gave me a position...How do I
    know it's the right one?!

397   TWO SHOT

> HEINRICH
> It is!
>
> PARKER
> We'll stay...Right here! And find
> out...There's still time - perhaps...
> if you'd like to change your mind.

Heinrich stares at Parker - speechless, white-faced.

> PARKER
> If you gave me a wrong location -
> just to save your own skin - it
> won't work. How about it?

Heinrich looks petrified; he glances involuntarily at the mockingly silent, immobile clock face...He tries to speak - but no sound comes out...The seconds tick by soundlessly.

Suddenly there is the distant thunder of an artillery battery firing a salvo! The men both start - and look up in apprehension.

398   CLOSEUP   HEINRICH

German - or American?

399   CLOSEUP   PARKER

Which battery fired??

400   TWO SHOT

And then there is the distinctive roar of several artillery shells passing overhead on their mission of destruction... Outgoing mail - <u>American</u> shells - headed for the 88's!

401   CLOSE SHOT   HEINRICH

His head goes down in defeat...

MATCH CUT TO:

<u>EXT. 88 BATTERY POSITION   NIGHT</u>

402   CLOSE SHOT   MAJOR SCHILLER

Startled, incredulous he looks up - and cries...

> SCHILLER
> Take cover!

130.

403   WIDE SHOT (STOCK)

The salvo hits just in front of the position.

EXT. U.S. ARTILLERY O.P. NIGHT

404   CLOSE SHOT   OBSERVER

He is looking through his field glasses; he has a phone in his hand.

                    OBSERVER
                    (on phone)
            Up one hundred...

EXT. U.S. ARTILLERY BATTERY POSITION   NIGHT

405   MED. SHOT   NON-COM

He is listening to a field phone, relaying the orders from the Observer.

                    NON-COM
           Up one hundred. Fire for effect!

VARIOUS STOCK SHOTS

406   A. U.S. Artillery Battery firing salvo after salvo...

       B. German 88 Battery being destroyed in an inferno of fire and erupting shell explosions...

INT. IPW ROOM OF SANTA MARIA SCHOOL HOUSE   NIGHT

407   TWO SHOT   HEINRICH, PARKER

Both physically and mentally exhausted they are listening to the distant thunder of the barrage...Heinrich walks to the desk and sinks down - burying his head in his arms...Parker watches him with a mixture of deep relief and compassion.

408   WIDER ANGLE

The door suddenly bursts open and Bradford, Armstrong, Hicks, Alvin and Sam come hurrying into the room. Bradford makes straight for Parker. Hicks - having made sure Parker is okay - goes to the clock.

409   TWO SHOT   BRADFORD, PARKER

                    BRADFORD
           You did it, boy! Good work!

132.

410 WIDER ANGLE   ACROSS BRADFORD AND PARKER IN F.G. TO CLOCK
    AND DOOR

   In the b.g. Armstrong and the two G.I.'s are leading
   Heinrich from the room; Bradford and Parker are watching.

                        PARKER
                      (quietly)
             He lived in the wrong place - at
             the wrong time...

411 ANOTHER ANGLE   FEATURING DOOR AND CLOCK

   Hicks frowning at the clock gives the weights a pull, and
   the pendulum a swing...and the clock begins to tick again.
   Then - just as Heinrich is being led past - he sets it at
   the correct time...a few seconds before midnight...And as
   Heinrich walks away, the chimes of the grandfather clock
   begin to STRIKE!

   Outside the sound of grinding, rumbling vehicles is HEARD,
   as the troops return for the offensive. Romeo appears in
   the doorway. Quickly he goes to Colonel Bradford and hands
   him a note. Bradford glances at it, and turns to Parker.

                        BRADFORD
             Okay, Dirk, coffee break's over!
             Corps's moving in. We're moving out!

EXT. SANTA MARIA VILLAGE SQUARE   NIGHT

412 WIDE SHOT

   The place is teeming with the orderly chaos of men, machines
   and equipment; the changeover is in progress; a major
   offensive is being mounted.

413 ANOTHER ANGLE   LONG SHOT

   Across the crowded village square a jeep is making its way
   in convoy with several other vehicles.

414 CLOSER ANGLE   JEEP

   Hicks is driving. Parker sits next to him - and in the back
   the big face of the grandfather clock sticks up!...Suddenly
   Parker raises himself up in the slowly moving jeep, and
   looks intently across the square.

415 LONG SHOT   POV PARKER

   On the far side of the crowded square a little band of
   people - armed to the teeth- are purposefully walking along
   in the opposite direction..Volpe, Tony, the Partisans - and Rina.

416 CLOSE SHOT PARKER

standing in the jeep. He calls:

                PARKER
Rina!...Rina!

417 MED. SHOT RINA

She turns towards the jeep - and a great, luminous smile suddenly shines on her lovely face.

418 MED. CLOSE SHOT PARKER

He contemplates jumping from the jeep and trying to make it across the square...but the jeep is being forced ahead, it cannot stop.

419 CLOSE SHOT RINA

She, too, is being forced along with the others by the sheer pressure of the crowd...She is looking back towards the disappearing jeep.

420 TWO SHOT PARKER, HICKS

Parker sinks down in the jeep dejectedly. Hicks glances at him.

                HICKS
War sure is hell! But cheer up,
Captain. She'll be okay. We'll
find her again. After all - we're
not in the Intelligence for nothing!

421 WIDER ANGLE

The crush of soldiers, equipment and vehicles presses the partisan band along going one way - Parker in the jeep going the other...And soon the two young people are out of sight of one another.

And CAMERA DRAWS UP AND BACK (BOOM SHOT) to a HIGH, WIDE SHOT of the village of Santa Maria...the square...the fountain...the school house...the farms...the teeming mass of men and machines...<u>ready to fight</u>!

                              FADE OUT:

<u>THE END</u>

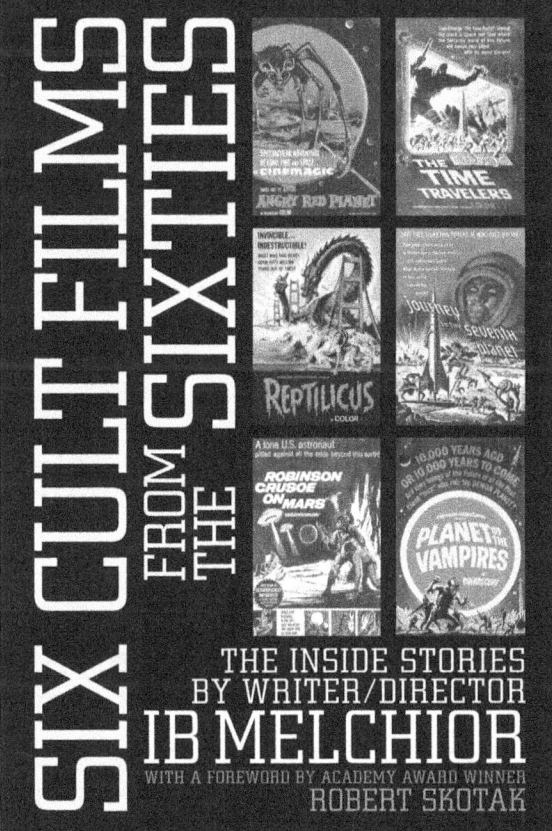

Bear Manor Media

Classic Cinema.
Timeless TV.
Retro Radio.

WWW.BEARMANORMEDIA.COM

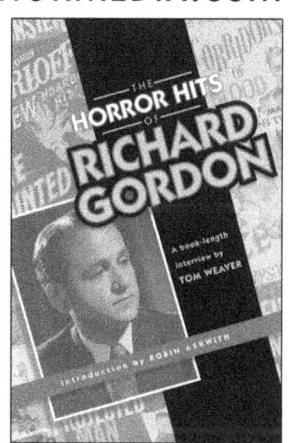